GEORGIAN DUBLIN

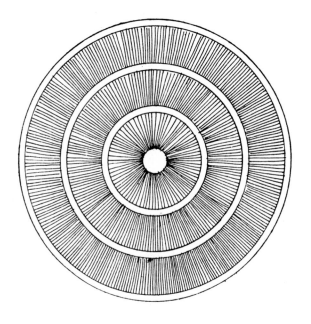

GEORGIAN DUBLIN

Desmond Guinness

B. T. BATSFORD LTD
LONDON

ENDPAPERS: *Béranger Toile of Lord Charlemont*

FRONTISPIECE *Bank of Ireland (Parliament House) after cleaning*

FIRST PUBLISHED 1979
COPYRIGHT DESMOND GUINNESS 1979

FILMSET AND PRINTED BY BAS PRINTERS LIMITED,
OVER WALLOP, HAMPSHIRE
FOR THE PUBLISHERS B. T. BATSFORD LTD,
4 FITZHARDINGE STREET, LONDON W1H OAH.
ISBN 0 7134 1908 3

Contents

Acknowledgments

The Author and Publishers would like to thank John Stewart who drew the plans in this book, and the following for the illustrations: A.C.L., for fig. 188; Aerofilms Ltd, for fig. 27; Country Life, for figs 122, 123, 124, 126, 127, 128, 129, 131, 132, 133, 134, 135, 136, 137, 138, 212, 215, 216, 219; Hugh Doran, for fig. 91; The Green Studio Ltd, for figs 1, 16, 29, 35, 48, 77, 80, 84, 90, 92, 94, 95, 155, 160, 166, 187a, 187b, 187c, 192, 211, 250, and the decorative drawings of coal hole covers on pages 1, 29, 115, 147; Arthur Guinness Son & Co (Dublin) Ltd, for fig. 63; J. and S. Harsch, for figs 2, 6, 7, 8, 9, 10, 11, 18, 31, 32, 34, 36, 37, 41, 42, 43, 46, 54, 65, 72, 75, 89, 93, 98, 99, 100, 104, 105, 109, 117, 118, 119, 121, 143, 145, 146, 147, 148, 149, 150, 151, 158, 159, 161, 162, 163, 164, 168, 171, 173, 178, 179, 196, 197, 202, 203, 209, 210, 221, 223, 224, 225, 226, 227, 229, 230, 231, 232, 233, 234, 236, 237, 238, 239, 243, 244, 245, 246, 247, 249; The Irish Georgian Society, for the frontispiece and figs 103, 177, 181, 182, 183, 184; The Irish Tourist Board—Bord Fáilte, for figs 19, 20, 24, 25, 26, 28, 38, 52, 58, 61, 62, 67, 68, 70, 74, 76, 85, 96, 97, 102, 108, 116, 120, 125, 130, 142, 153, 165, 167, 170, 174, 175, 185, 186, 193, 204, 207, 235, 240, 241, 242; The National Gallery of Ireland, for fig. 81; National Parks and Monuments Branch, Office of Public Works in Ireland, for figs 3, 22, 23, 45, 47, 51, 59, 60, 107, 111, 139, 190, 194a, 194b, 195, 198, 199, 200, 205, 206, 222, 228; Tony O'Malley Pictures Ltd, for fig. 63; Pieterse-Davison International Ltd, for figs 30, 50, 88; Walter Pfeiffer, for fig. 5; Rex Roberts Studio Ltd, for fig. 152; P. Rossinore, for fig. 140; the Royal Hospital, Kilmainham, for fig. 112; Ryan, for figs 33, 44, 49, 53, 55, 56, 64, 66, 78, 79, 82, 83, 86, 87, 101, 106, 110, 113, 114, 115, 144, 154, 169, 176, 201, 208, 213, 217; Ulster Museum, Belfast, for fig. 57; J. W. Walker & Son Ltd, Organ Builders, for fig. 152; Bestick Williams, Dublin, for figs 21, 69, 71, 73. Many thanks also to Mark Molony (research) and Peter Curran.

For Penny

Introduction

Georgian Dublin has many hidden beauties. Behind the orderly brick façades, un-Irish in their sober regularity, there are some interiors of astonishing beauty. Very few of the Georgian town houses are still kept up in any style. The motor car has taken the more affluent citizens out to the suburbs, leaving a vacuum that has been filled by offices, stores and religious institutions. Although any use is better than none, these houses were built for people and an elegant way of life, not for office equipment and fluorescent lighting. When Dublin became a capital once more, there was a chance that some of the great town houses might have come to life again as foreign embassies, but most of these were established in Ballsbridge, a Victorian suburb reminiscent of North Oxford. Not one of the great town houses is furnished in period and open to the public, and considering the lack of official pride in them it is fortunate that so many have survived intact.

Georgian Dublin has been preserved by a cocoon of poverty, by being a backwater in terms of European currents, and the new Ireland is fortunate to have such a fine capital. There are those, however, who feel that it is not really Irish. They are unable to disassociate the architecture from the corrupt and vicious system of government that was imposed on Ireland at precisely the time the city was being built, and cannot appreciate it dispassionately as a work of art.

The Battle of the Boyne in 1690 re-established the power of the Protestant Ascendancy, and Georgian Dublin owes its face to the Anglo-Irish aristocracy. Considered Irish in England and English in Ireland, the Ascendancy was a small élite, and the native Irish, who had clung to the old faith and spoke another language, had no feelings of loyalty towards them. These native Irish were in any case not city-dwellers, nor did they build along the coast. It was the Vikings who established trading ports around the shores of Ireland, from the eighth century onwards, and Dublin was one of them. These Viking ports were in turn taken by the Normans after 1170. Dublin owed its origin to foreigners and was for centuries a foreign citadel within its defensive walls.

'It is easy to see', the poet Lord Dunsany wrote of Dublin, 'that a great race has passed through it'. It was indeed great in terms of the legacy of art and architecture that it left behind, as this book attempts to show. It is a sobering thought to consider the quantity of Irish silver, glass, furniture, paintings and so on that has left the city, and the country too for that matter, since the eighteenth century.

The flight from Dublin began in 1801 when the Act of Union became law. The Irish parliament was abolished and the country was governed direct from

Westminster. The silver lining crossed to England, leaving a dark cloud hanging over the city, which burst into flaming rebellion a hundred years later.

Sir John Mahaffy, Provost of Trinity College, founded the Georgian Society in 1908 for the purpose of recording the best Georgian houses and their interiors, many of which had degenerated into lodging houses and slums. He must have realised that the life of these buildings was soon to be cut short. The Society was to last for five years and publish five volumes of photographs accompanied by scholarly research. The first four are concerned with Dublin, and the fifth volume is devoted to the principal Irish country houses. After the five volumes had appeared and the Georgian Society had come to an end, the interest in the architecture and decoration of the period that Mahaffy had engendered resulted in a sixth volume, 'Georgian Mansions in Ireland'. The authors, Thomas Sadleir and Page Dickinson, had both been involved with the Georgian Society publications and, as its name implies, this too deals with country houses. The first five volumes were re-printed by the Irish University Press in 1970, but as there was copyright on the sixth volume it was left out of this modern edition, and has become the rarest of them all.

The Georgian Society was no doubt dismayed that the future of the buildings with which it was concerned was in jeopardy, but it was not a preservation society; its purpose was to make a record. 'It requires no intimate knowledge of Dublin to perceive that it is not a provincial town, but a fading capital', wrote Mahaffy in his preface to Volume I. 'But, alas! most of these monuments of a brilliant society are doomed to decay and disappearance; many have already vanished.' It is remarkable that in spite of the pressures of the twentieth century, when Dublin became a capital once more, so much has survived. The 1916 rebellion wreaked havoc in O'Connell Street, since rebuilt in 'neon-Georgian' and the General Post Office went up in flames at this time. The Custom House and the Four Courts were destroyed during the Civil War and rebuilt almost exactly as they had been; their interiors, however, are now of little interest. That of the Four Courts had been very fine, and it is hard to imagine Beresford's apartments in the Custom House having been devoid of ornament.

Many of the great public buildings are resplendent now after cleaning. These are of stone, framed by the reticent brick terraces which are plain to the point of monotony and provide as it were a brick continuo for these great stone fanfares. It is the uniformity of street and square in Dublin that gives the city its character. The unending succession of cliff-like terraces gain their effect from this plainness. *The Commissioners for Making Wide and Convenient Streets*, to give them their full title, were formed in 1757. They were given the power to make compulsory purchase orders, pay compensation and drive new streets through the older parts of the city. They were able to ease the circulation of traffic, open up vistas, and improve the approaches to bridges and squares.

There was no attempt at formal, pilastered squares as are found in Edinburgh and Bath. The starkly modern effect conveyed by engravings was softened by the fact that Dublin was a country town, and the jangle of harness would mingle with the forlorn lowing of cattle on their way to market. James

Malton, in 1790, depicted the Parliament House with a couple of pigs being driven past it. He must have realised that this would give offence, and in his final version of the aquatint in 1793, the pigs have been erased while the dog still barks and the driver wields his stick in thin air.

There was a healthy rivalry between the developments to the north and south of the River Liffey. The Viceregal Court held sway in Dublin Castle on the south side, where the old medieval walled city had stood. The two cathedrals and Trinity College were here also. The grandest early eighteenth-century houses, however, were built in Henrietta Street on the north side where by 1800 the Gardiner Estate had spread its tentacles over a huge area, including Rutland (now Parnell) Square and Mountjoy Square. The original scheme for Mountjoy Square is illustrated here. In the middle was to have been

1. Original project for Mountjoy Square, by Thomas Sherrard, 1787

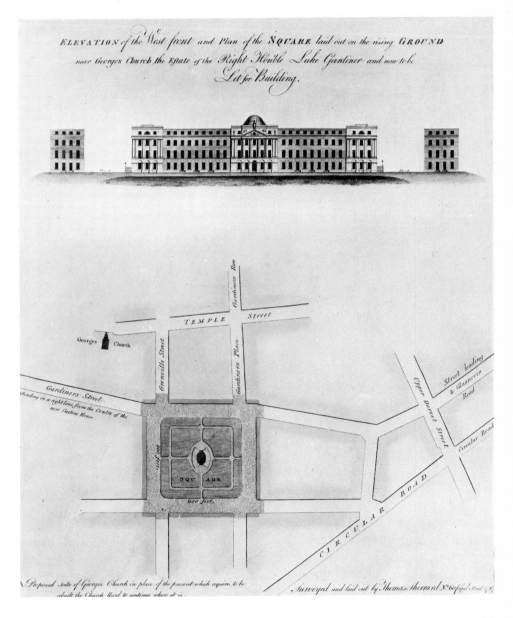

ELEVATION of the West front and Plan of the SQUARE laid out on the rising GROUND near Georges Church the Estate of the Right Hon'ble Luke Gardiner and now to be Let for Building.

a new church, St. George's, which was eventually built close by in Hardwicke Crescent. Each side of the square was to have had a central dome and a pediment surmounting a frontispiece with giant pilasters dominated by a statue and urns. Dublin would have had a formal square akin to Charlotte Square in Edinburgh, but instead the scheme was dropped in favour of plain frontages.

The late seventeenth-century skyline of the city was jagged like the teeth of a saw. The houses were built after the Dutch pattern with their gable ends fronting the street, sometimes quite elaborately fashioned with primitive scrollwork. William of Orange is said to have introduced the sash window and the use of brick to Ireland. Some brick was indeed imported from Holland as ballast although Irish-made brick had been in use as far back as the Viceroyalty of Strafford. String courses of brick were often found at each floor level. These early houses had corner fireplaces and simple wainscotting of oak, or pine stained to simulate oak, with wooden 'boxed' cornices, bolection mouldings, and window seats. The fireplaces had little or no mantel shelf, and were an extension of the panelling. They were usually plain or adorned with a simple shell. Free-standing basket grates were the successors of the fire dogs of the seventeenth century. The tall, narrow doors were of oak, with panels divided up the centre, and drop handles of brass. The three-pane windows with their heavy glazing bars were almost flush with the outside wall, and there was no projecting sill.

As a measure of safety, external shutters were sometimes found on the ground floor, as there was no area protecting the house from the street, and thus no railings. The hallway was no more than a passage leading through to the narrow stairs with barley-sugar banisters. Almost all these houses have gone, although in Molesworth Street there are some gabled houses that were subsequently concealed behind a straight parapet. Their early date is betrayed by the spacing of the windows on the top floor. The contents of these houses was simple and they were too small for elaborate entertaining.

In the 1730s grander houses came to be built, and mahogany was introduced for the first time. Strictly speaking, oak gave way to walnut and walnut to mahogany. Being cheaper, pine was dressed up as one or the other, but never revealed its true character with 'warts and all' as is fashionable today. Dark mahogany provided the perfect anchor for the plaster flourishes which were to decorate walls and ceilings with ever-increasing virtuosity. Richard Castle, the German architect (*fl.* 1729–51), favoured it and if his houses were considered gloomy and old-fashioned by the end of the century this may have been one of the reasons. Because it was expensive its use was confined to doors and their surrounds, stairs, and panelling up to the level of the dado only. As oak gives way to mahogany the proportions change and doors become wider and less high, with panels running across them. Mahogany in turn gives way to painted timber surfaces, and for reasons of economy, hard woods are no longer used except for the doors themselves. The cornice often provides a clue to the dating of a house. In the late seventeenth century timber cornices were used that were an extension of the panelling and hardly crossed on to the ceiling at all. These gave way to plaster cornices *c.* 1725 which were fairly heavy and took

2. *No. 6 Parnell Square*

3. *Ardee House, Ardee Street*

4. LEFT *No. 9 Henrietta Street*
5. *No. 20 Molesworth Street*

13

6. No. 40 Lower Dominick Street

7. No. 27 Molesworth Street

8. Nos 60 and 61 Blessington Street

10. Nos 14 and 15 Usher's Island

9. No. 11 Parnell Square

11. No. 17 Harcourt Street

up as much of the ceiling as of the wall, often as much as eighteen inches in a high room. The cornice remained at forty-five degrees until the end of the century, but became much smaller in size. A cornice projecting a mere six inches or less is often found during the Adam period even where the room is high, and at the same time the chair-rail will drop to a mere three feet above the floor. After 1800 the cornice leaves the wall almost completely and creeps across to frame the ceiling, completing its upward progression.

By the 1740s marble mantelpieces of a bolder and more architectonic variety were introduced, providing a focal point for the room, and the corner fireplace gradually disappeared. There is an extensive range of native marbles in Ireland, which can be seen complete with key in the hallway of the Office of Public Works, 51 St. Stephen's Green, which was at one time the Museum of Irish Industry. Siena marble was very popular and had to be imported, and there is no native white marble. Green Connemara marble was not used until the Celtic revival of the late nineteenth century. The Dublin Society (which became Royal in 1821) awarded premiums for the best carved plaques for mantels; these sometimes related to the theme of decoration of the room. In the Adam period mantels became more delicate and less dominant. The inlaid work of Pietro Bossi commands high prices today, and has been much imitated. He invented a mixture of glue and powdered marble whereby subtle shades of colour could be inlaid on a white background, but he took his secret to the grave with him. In the early nineteenth century, a more masculine variety of mantel was favoured, with a shelf wide enough to accommodate the household clock. Often the wide shelf is added, and the old mantel left *in situ*; in Victorian times a purple fringe would occasionally be found necessary to conceal the delicate form of some innocent nymph. It is easy to remove a mantel, and hundreds of them have been sold out of the houses to which they belong – the process of removing plasterwork is highly complicated, which is indeed fortunate.

The use of imported coal in Dublin households after 1750 called for a smaller fireplace, less wasteful of the heat, than the free-standing dog grate. In many cases the opening was filled in, and square brass surrounds substituted, often finely engraved and signed by the Dublin maker.

Windows were universally glazed with three panes across, their height diminishing towards the parapet. Glazing bars became narrower and more attenuated as the eighteenth century progressed until with the invention of plate glass at the beginning of Victoria's reign they vanished altogether. Sometimes the basement windows, or those at the back of the house, will retain heavy sashes while those facing the street will have been altered to suit the prevailing fashion. Six-inch reveals, painted white, became standard in 1730 and remained so for a hundred years. The parapet and window sills are usually of granite.

The typical Dublin house façade changed little during the Georgian period. From about 1730 the doorways were of the architectural variety, and the front hall was lit by a window. Lighting the hall from a fanlight above the door was common in 1750, although the more elaborate fanlights of the peacock-tail variety date from 1770–90. The hall was paved in stone, often in black and white squares. An area protected from the

12. No. 9 Henrietta Street

13.
13 Henrietta Street

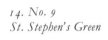

14. No. 9 St. Stephen's Green

15. Bossi mantelpiece formerly at 20 North Great George's Street (see also fig. 178)

street by iron railings gave light to the kitchens in the basement. Coal and timber were stored in cellars beneath the pavement. The dining room and an office or study were on the ground floor, and the main reception rooms were on the *piano nobile* above, away from the noise and smell of the street. A great deal of time was thus spent on the main staircase which ended on the floor above street level. A secondary staircase, more utilitarian in character, led from basement to attic. The grand staircases of Dublin deserve a book of their own; the plasterer was here permitted to indulge his wildest fantasies.

The Georgian terraced houses were built in groups of two or three. A tenant would lease enough ground to build a house for himself and one or two more beside it which would be let: the houses for letting tend to have plainer interiors. The town houses of the great nobles were, like the public buildings, built of stone. Leinster House, Tyrone House, Newman House, Powerscourt House, Charlemont House, and Aldborough House are among those still standing. Only the Provost's House at Trinity College is in use as it was originally intended. A good collection of Irish Georgian furniture may be seen in the echoing Victorian museum in Kildare Street, but it would look happier displayed in one of these houses. The great drawing rooms are frequently divided up with incongruous partitions, equipped with modern desks, strip-lighting and linoleum. The paintwork is brown and cream, and where the decoration includes the human figure, it will be painted in shiny 'natural' colours, resembling the corpse at an American leave-taking.

Plasterwork

Glimpses of splendid ceilings in upstairs drawing rooms will be seen by those who walk the streets at night. Between 1725 and 1830, while the exterior of the Dublin town house only changed in minor detail, five distinct styles of plaster decoration were used.

1   *The compartmented ceiling, 1725–40.* The division of ceilings into geometrical patterns—squares, ovals, circles and oblongs—derives from the very earliest plaster ornament which was an attempt to disguise or decorate the beams supporting the floor above. To 'ceil' or seal with plaster was originally a means of keeping out the draught, hence 'ceiling'.

2   *Baroque and rococo decoration, 1740–1760.* The Italian brothers, Paul and Philip Francini, were the first to introduce the human figure into plaster decoration in other than a primitive fashion. Their best known work in Ireland is at Carton, Co. Kildare, where the great saloon ceiling, representing the Courtship of the Gods, dates from 1739. It is less well known that in 1740 they executed a version of this baroque ceiling in Dublin, in the saloon of No. 85 St. Stephen's Green, now a part of Newman House. The Francini work at No. 9 St. Stephen's Green can be dated 1756, and it was repeated three years later at Castletown, another great house in Co. Kildare, except that in the country house the elaborate frames are empty, avoiding the rather over-crowded effect

LABORE ET VIRTUTE GLORIA

The Bricklayers & Plasterers Arms

16. *Arms of the Guild of Plasterers and Bricklayers from* Brooking's Map of Dublin, *1728*
17. RIGHT *Compartmented ceiling, No. 9 Henrietta Street*
18. *Francini ceiling, No. 9 St. Stephen's Green*

19. Robert West plasterwork, No. 20 Lower Dominick Street
20. RIGHT
Plasterwork, Belvedere House
21. FACING PAGE
Greek revival plasterwork, King's Inns library

at No. 9. One other Italian, and only one, is known to have worked in Dublin. He was commissioned by Dr. Mosse of the Rotunda Hospital to decorate the chapel there in 1755. Bartholomew Cramillion was his name, and it was his only commission in Ireland. Apart from him, and the Francini brothers, the stuccodores whose work found such brilliant expression in Dublin at this period were Irish, although all stucco ornament is still thought to have been the work of 'Eye'talian craftsmen. The principal native exponent of the craft was Robert West, who had the contract for all the plastering in the Rotunda Hospital apart from the chapel, and is presumed to have watched Cramillion at work.

West is known for the plaster birds he loved to model; at No. 20 Lower Dominick Street (1755) they are almost free-standing, perched on asymmetrical rococo pedestals which grow naturally out of the wall decoration. At No. 86 St. Stephen's Green the birds are far from peaceably disposed, and seem about to swoop down in a vicious attack on those mounting the staircase. In both these houses the principal work is on the way up to the main reception rooms. Decoration that would have been overpowering in the drawing room was evidently acceptable on staircase walls and ceilings.

In 1757 Sir Edward Barry built himself a villa, Mespil House, which has been demolished but whose plasterwork was of such high quality that it has been transferred to the President's House in the Phoenix Park and to Dublin Castle. The identity of the artist remains a mystery, but it is certain that he also worked at Belvedere, Co. Westmeath, a house of the same date which is still intact, and at the La Touche Bank in Castle Street. The La Touche ceiling, representing 'Venus blessée par l'amour', was also saved when the building was torn down, and it has been installed in the Bank of Ireland on College Green. The soft and graceful modelling was more subtle than that of the Francini or indeed anyone else.

Robert West had a large school of followers and apprentices, who were responsible for much of the work that is attributed to him. The standard was high, and plasterwork that is in any way crude or primitive is seldom found in Dublin. The same cannot be said for country districts where, especially in the lesser houses, coarse modelling in antiquated style is found. Where this work gains over its more sophisticated counterpart in Dublin is in crispness, because in the clean country air it has not been found necessary to smother it in layers of paint.

3 Transitional, 1760–80. The dead hand of Adam put an end to rococo flights of fancy, and decoration gradually froze in the icy grip of the neo-classical movement associated with his name. Neither Adam, Chambers or Wyatt came to Ireland, but all three designed interiors for Dublin.

Robert Adam's only Dublin interior was designed for Lord Langford's house in Mary Street, but has not survived. In 1762 Sir William Chambers designed Lord Charlemont's town house, which dominates Parnell Square, having already started work on the Marino Casino at Clontarf for the same patron. The long gallery at Leinster House, where the Senate now sits, was remodelled by James Wyatt in 1780. The taste for rococo and free-hand expression also managed to survive during this period. Powerscourt House, South William Street, dates from 1771 and both styles are represented here under the same roof. In country districts taste was slow to change, and rococo survived well into the '70s.

4 Neo-Classical, 1780–1800. An extensive use of repetitive moulds made the plasterwork at the end of the eighteenth century somewhat monotonous. These were used over and again in different houses by the exponents of the Adam style. Angelica Kauffmann, Peter de Gree and others provided paintings which could be incorporated into these geometrical schemes as an alternative to plaster plaques. The work of Michael Stapleton, who inherited Robert West's practice, and like West was an architect as well as a stuccodore, stands out as the best of this period. Although Stapleton made use of moulds, there is freehand work also, and his sense of spacing was impeccable. Low relief plasterwork of this period can look well picked out in bright colours, whereas figured work in high relief should be left white; above all, 'natural' colours, such as flesh tints, should be avoided.

Adamesque decoration often covered the walls as well as the ceiling, and was not popular with those who had returned from the Grand Tour laden with pictures. It demanded furniture of its own period, as anything earlier looked clumsy and old-fashioned, another disadvantage. It was considered effeminate, suitable for a boudoir, and the style died a natural death after 1800.

5   *The Greek and Gothic Revivals, 1800–30.* After the Act of Union in 1801 there was a return to stronger, more masculine plasterwork associated with the Greek and Gothic revivals. This is found in public buildings, as town houses of architectural interest were no longer being built. Frederick Darley's Kings Inns library (1827) has a giant double-acanthus in the ceiling, and Francis Johnston's St. George's Church (1802) is in his individualistic version of the Greek. Johnston also worked in the perpendicular Gothic style, and one of the more flamboyant neo-Gothic essays in Dublin is to be found at the Church of the Most Holy Trinity (1807) in Dublin Castle, formerly the Chapel Royal (p. 52).

Religion

Georgian Dublin was a Protestant city and its institutions, from Trinity College to schools, hospitals and trade guilds, came under the patronage of the Church of Ireland. Although today ninety per cent of the population is Catholic, the Catholics have to make do with a nineteenth-century Pro-Cathedral while the Church of Ireland has clung on to both the medieval cathedrals, Christ Church and St. Patrick's, each complete with choir school. Beside this there are twelve Protestant churches still in use. Some of these are of great importance from the historical and architectural standpoint. They contain marble memorials, organs, carved woodwork, silver, fonts and so forth of great artistic value. The best of them are situated in the heart of the city, but the population has been moving away from the centre for many years. As a result there are few worshippers on a Sunday morning, and these churches are becoming redundant. The Catholic churches in the centre of Dublin have also been affected by the move to new housing estates outside the city, and although they are still crowded, fewer masses are now being said, and there has been a reduction in the number of clergy. It is unlikely therefore that they would wish to take on any of the unwanted Protestant churches, and their future is a matter of concern.

The chapel of Trinity College has now become ecumenical: the Rotunda and Dr. Steevens' Hospital both still have Protestant chapels. The Chapel Royal in Dublin Castle, and the chapel in the grounds of the former Hibernian Military School in Phoenix Park (now St. Mary's Chest Hospital) have become Catholic. The Royal Hospital, Kilmainham, has a vast seventeenth-century chapel with an elaborate Carolean ceiling, albeit a papier-mâché replica of the original. It has been de-consecrated and closed. The hospital itself, a monumental symbol of Protestant Dublin, is to be restored and used as a conference centre.

The army barracks were equipped with both Protestant and Catholic chapels for the Dublin garrison, and at church parade the troops were divided according to faith. The Church of Ireland (Protestant) services are of the low variety, but by continental standards the Catholic services are also low. Except where Victorian glass has been inserted, the Protestant church of the Georgian period has the cheerful aspect of an assembly room. Gothic revival churches of both denominations are illustrated here. In country districts, when the Protestants favoured one style of building the Catholics would choose another. As far as Dublin is concerned, however, the Gothic Revival was taken up by both churches simultaneously, and in much the same way.

STREETSCAPES

22. Sweeney's Lane

23. RIGHT
No. 51 St. Stephen's Green

24. Harcourt Terrace

Preservation

Most of the major public buildings are resplendent after their recent cleaning, and have recaptured the elegance of a Malton print. Before the face-lift began the façades were enhanced by being soot black in some places and rainwashed white in others; they will, unfortunately, soon go an even grey. They have taken on a pale golden hue, akin to Bath, very different from the stern aspect of twenty years ago. The great masterpieces are well cared for; the preservation of less important buildings is left to chance. Even buildings on List One, the top grade for preservation, have been pulled down and no penalty has been incurred. No law as yet exists to protect the interior of buildings even if they are on this list. As a result the finest early eighteenth-century staircase, in Lisle House, Molesworth Street, and the finest Victorian one, in the former Kildare Street Club, have both been recently destroyed. To preserve the façade of Lisle House at the expense of the interior is better than nothing, but in this case the barley-sugar staircase and contemporary panelling were of particular interest. These staircases took up an enormous amount of space. In houses that became tenements, whole families would be squeezed in at the expense of the main staircase, as at No. 13 Henrietta Street. Poverty was, however, to destroy less of Dublin than prosperity. The staircases in Molesworth Street and Kildare Street were both destroyed by prosperous concerns, and the planning authority was powerless. When two or three of the terraced houses fall into the same ownership today, it generally means the end. The developer will do anything to get them down as quickly as possible, working from the inside behind closed shutters, or at weekends, so that by the time anyone is aware it is too late. Cement, steel and glass office blocks have resulted, a vile intrusion on the streetscape. Georgian Dublin covers only five per cent of the city's extent and could be preserved if the laws were amended. As it is, the developers are eager to get in to this part of town, while a large part of Dublin lies derelict, in need of good modern development.

Infill

The uniformity of the façades of Georgian Dublin cries out for their replacement in the same vein, when this becomes necessary. Attempts at infill that are an affront to good architectural mores are too often found. Horizontal balconies in Lower Gardiner Street, plate-glass pastiche in Molesworth and Kildare Streets and black buildings that suck the light out of the street—these add nothing to the beauty of the city. A bold attempt to rehabilitate some of the crumbling Georgian houses in the Summerhill/Gardiner Street area was initiated in the 1940s. Houses were rebuilt in Georgian style to provide new flats and improve housing conditions without the breaking up of neighbourhoods. The idea was good, but the scheme pleased no-one. The detail was poor, the white reveals so essential to enliven the streetscape were lacking, the windows were painted brown, and the fanlights were unglazed. The brick is an

25. Victorian houses, Mount Pleasant Square, Rathmines

unsubtle shade of red, giving a machine-made look. The flats proved expensive to build and inconvenient to live in. Condemnation of them was unanimous, and as a result Georgian pastiche earned a bad name, although the Cement Building on Fitzwilliam Square/Upper Pembroke Street has for long stood as an example of what can be done. It is in the Georgian tradition to leave the design of the interior to the whim of the owner; saving or reproducing the façade is next best to saving the entire building. It mattered not at all to the Wide Streets Commissioners what sort of interior was given to a particular house, so long as the façade conformed. Occasionally the front of one of the Dublin town houses has to be refaced, because the brick has perished, and this can be done without difficulty.

The rot set in in 1963 when the Electricity Supply Board decided to pull down sixteen houses in a row in Lower Fitzwilliam Street, which were part of a Georgian vista over half a mile in length. The houses were rotten, inconvenient and unsuitable for offices. They should have been put on the market and sold to people who would appreciate them. Sir John Summerson was brought over from England and pronounced them 'architectural rubbish; a rotten, uneven series'. Sir Albert Richardson spoke up for the case of preservation, but to no avail: down they came, to be replaced by a modern block of unfortunate aspect, already too small for its purpose. The architectural students took the side of the vandals, and picketed the meeting organised to save the houses. 'Dublin must not be a museum. We want a living city with modern buildings', their banners read. The students have now changed their tune, and are at the forefront of the fight to save old buildings in the city. In both Hume Street and Upper Pembroke Street they moved in when demolition began, and won the day. The Dublin Civic Group, formed in 1965 by Professor Kevin B. Nowlan, examines all planning applications that come before the Corporation, and where necessary, lodges objections in order to preserve interiors, streetscape and skyline. The more that is lost in terms of the architecture, the more conscious the citizens of Dublin are becoming of their heritage. This book will have served its purpose if it comes as a revelation to those who have so far taken that heritage for granted.

PUBLIC BUILDINGS

The Blue Coat School, Blackhall Place

The Blue Coat School or King's Hospital has recently moved out to Palmerstown, Co. Dublin, where there are better facilities for sport. Their old buildings in the city have been acquired by the Incorporated Law Society and are in the process of being restored. These were designed by Thomas Ivory in 1773, but for reasons of economy a squat dome was erected over the central block, a poor substitute for the elegant spire intended by the architect. The northern wing contains the former chapel, which was considered already in 1818 to be lighted 'perhaps too strongly for the solemnity of religious worship'. The southern wing contained the dining hall, and above there was a dormitory. Institutions of the period tended to have plain interiors concealed behind elaborate frontages. The Board Room here, however, has an elaborate plaster ceiling by Charles Thorp, stylistically older than the building. The former Blue Coat School is one of the least known of Dublin's public buildings, being tucked away at the back of the quays north of the river, not far from the entrance to Phoenix Park.

26. Blue Coat School

Dublin Bridges from West to East

Island Bridge (Sarah Bridge) by Alexander Stephen(son) 1794
Sean Heuston Bridge (King's Bridge) by George Papworth 1827
Rory O'More Bridge (Barrack Bridge) 1863
Queen Maev Bridge (Queen's Bridge) by General Charles Vallancey 1764
Fr. Mathew Bridge (Whitworth Bridge) by George Knowles 1816
O'Donovan Rossa Bridge (Richmond Bridge) by J. Savage 1813
Grattan Bridge (on the *site* of Essex Bridge) 1874
Liffey Bridge (Wellington or Iron or Metal or Halfpenny Bridge) 1816
O'Connell Bridge (Carlisle Bridge) by James Gandon (widened 1880) 1791
Butt Bridge
Matthew Talbot Bridge 1977

27. View of Dublin from the south, dominated by the Four Courts (Photograph: Aerofilms)

28. RIGHT *Looking across Liffey Bridge at Christ Church Cathedral*

Broadstone Station

The Broadstone terminal has been closed since 1931 and is now used by the State transport company as offices and stores. It was designed in the Egyptian style by J. S. Mulvany, 1841–50, and the line to Mullingar was first opened to traffic in 1849. A colonnade, two hundred and eighty feet in length, which provided shelter for the jarveys and their cabs, was added in 1861.

29. Broadstone Station

The City Hall – *formerly The Royal Exchange*

Thomas Cooley was the winner of the architectural competition instituted by a committee of Dublin merchants in 1769 for building a Royal Exchange at the head of Parliament Street. The earliest neo-classical public building in the city, it has served as the City Hall since 1852, when it became the administrative centre of Dublin Corporation. The main hall has changed little in two hundred years, apart from Victorian tiles and an unfortunate mosaic frieze, and provides an elegant space for sculpture. The divergence of scale between the figures on display detracts from their individual merit. The statue of Dr. Charles Lucas, who was instrumental in financing the building, was carved by Edward Smyth when the sculptor was aged only 23, and originally stood in a niche on the staircase. Its pedestal has a bas-relief representing Liberty, seated, with her rod and cap. The City Hall has recently been cleaned and windows with panes have been installed, greatly to the credit of Dublin Corporation.

City Hall, ground floor

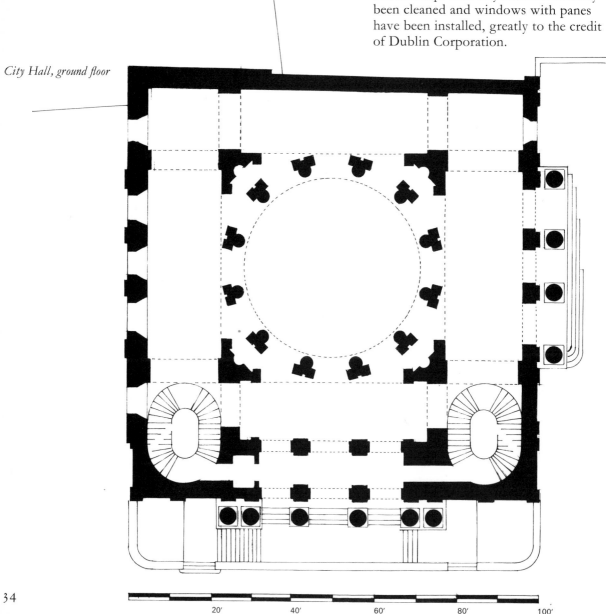

20'   40'   60'   80'   100'

30. ABOVE LEFT *City Hall*

31. LEFT *City Hall ceiling and frieze*

32. ABOVE *Edward Smyth's statue of Dr. Charles Lucas in the City Hall*

The College of Surgeons, St. Stephen's Green

Edward Parke's three-bay pedimented building, begun in 1806, was later enlarged by four bays to the north and the pediment re-centred by William Murray in 1825. The tympanum contains the Royal Arms and statues of Esculapius, Hygeia and Minerva dominate the pediment, the work of John Smyth, son of Edward. The elaborate interior contains some fine sculpture.

33. BELOW *College of Surgeons façade*

34. *College of Surgeons entrance hall. Central statue is of William Dease (d. 1798), one of the founders of the College; on the left is Sir Philip Crampton, and on the right Richard Carmichael*

Collins Barracks – *formerly Royal Barracks*

Thomas Burgh was appointed Surveyor General in 1700 and in 1701 he obtained his first and largest commission, the Royal Barracks, which had room for four regiments of foot and four of horse. The parade grounds were called Cavalry Square, Royal Square, Palatine Square and Brunswick Square. The massive granite façades of Royal Square are three storeys over stocky rusticated arcades, whose vaulted ceilings must have added to the echoes from the parade ground. In 1887, the health authorities insisted on the removal of the corners of Palatine Square to give more air, as the soldiers were said to be prone to fainting. The Barracks were handed over to the National Army in 1922 and renamed in honour of Michael Collins.

35. Granite façade of Collins Barracks

36. Vaulted arcades, Collins Barracks

37. The Rutland Memorial, Collins Barracks

The Custom House

James Gandon, an English architect, was summoned to Dublin by the Rt. Hon. John Beresford in 1781, for the purpose of building a new Custom House. The old one had stood on Essex Quay in the heart of the city, and had been designed by Thomas Burgh in 1707. A new site was chosen on marshy ground north of the river, and nearly a mile closer to its mouth. The building was fraught with difficulties and intrigue, and securing proper foundations proved complicated and expensive. Beresford, who provided himself with apartments in the new building, came in for more criticism than the architect, but even Gandon carried a 'good cane sword . . . determined to defend myself to the last' on his visits to inspect the works.

Most of the carved ornament is by Edward Smyth; in the pediment are Britannia and Hibernia embracing, and emblems of Liberty and Peace. Smyth also carved the Royal Arms at each of the four corners, and his best known works here are the Riverine Heads set in as keystones above doors and windows on the ground floor. Dr. Harold Leask has established the identity of these heads, although there is still uncertainty regarding the Nore and the Barrow. Starting with the keystone over the main door facing the river, the only female head in the series, and going to the right they are as follows:

1 Liffey
2 Boyne (1690)
3 Barrow (?)
4 Blackwater
5 Atlantic Ocean
6 Bann
7 Shannon
8 Lee (centre, rear elevation)
9 Lagan
10 Suir
11 Nore (?)
12 Slaney
13 Foyle (1689)
14 Erne (to the left of the Liffey)

Custom House, ground floor

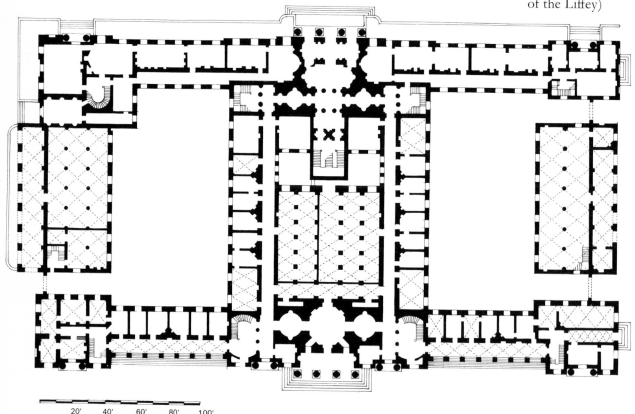

20'   40'   60'   80'   100'

38. *The Custom House*

39. *(a) Liffey*
    (b) Foyle

a

b

41

40. Custom House from the east

Gandon was a pupil of Sir William Chambers and similar carved ornament is to be found at Somerset House on the Thames, designed by Chambers. His Marino Casino, Clontarf, and the Custom House both have funereal urns on the parapet; at the Casino they function as chimneys.

The rear elevation echoes the main front but has no pediment. Instead there are four statues by Banks representing the four corners of the globe. Until the elevated railway was built, there was a vista of Georgian houses nearly a mile long up Gardiner Street, framed by the crescent named Beresford Place, sadly depleted now.

The Custom House was burned by the Republican forces during the Civil War in 1921, and rebuilt. The stone used on the peristyle is Irish Ardbraccan limestone, a shade darker than the Portland stone of the original. The immense statue of Commerce by Smyth is still on her lofty pedestal crowning the dome, and no doubt proud that the whole building has been cleaned.

Dr. Steevens' Hospital, Steevens' Lane

Dr. Steevens' Hospital was built 1721–1733 and designed by Thomas Burgh, architect of the great library at Trinity College. There is an arcaded courtyard, a steeply pitched roof and dormer windows. Burgh died before it was completed; Sir Edward Lovett Pearce succeeded him as Surveyor General and was responsible for the completion of the building. Pearce designed the Worth Library, now used as the hospital boardroom, to contain the four thousand books that were bequeathed by Edward Worth. Hu: Wilson was paid £8 6s od for the 'two large Corinthian Columns with the pedestals' in 1735. Between these columns, over the mantel, is a full-length portrait of Dr. Worth, and in a row of portraits above the books there hangs one of the foundress, Grizel Steevens, holding a more elaborate design for the hospital than was carried out. She was the sister of Dr. Richard Steevens whose estate was left in her care to be devoted to the founding of a hospital.

The arcades are of local limestone painted over, which would look better with the paint removed. The walls are of rubble plastered. The rooms across the corners in the quadrangle are a nineteenth-century addition and the chapel, still in use, is modern.

Dr. Steevens' Hospital

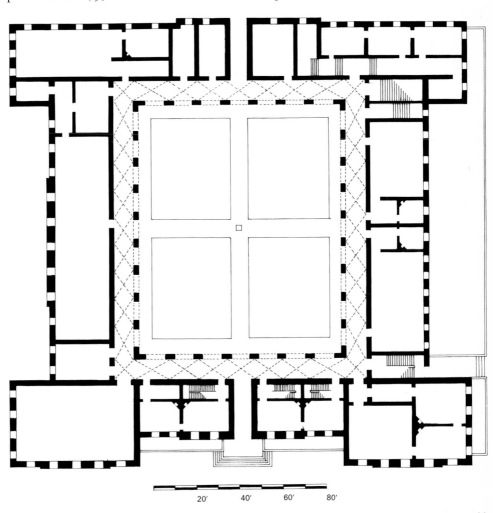

20'   40'   60'   80'

41. *Courtyard, Dr. Steevens' Hospital*

42. BELOW *Worth Library, Dr. Steevens' Hospital*
43. RIGHT *Portrait of Edward Worth, M.D. (1678–1733), Trustee and Governor of the Hospital*

44. Plaque above gateway to Dr. Steevens' Hospital, commemorates Dr. Richard Steevens and his sister Grizel Steevens

Dublin Castle

There is scarcely a trace of the old Dublin Castle, built by the Anglo-Normans *c.* 1200, whose walls lie hidden now behind serene brick façades. The gentle scale and texture of the buildings, which comprise an upper and a lower yard, are reminiscent of a university quad. Yet for close on seven centuries from the time of its completion Dublin Castle was the centre of government in Ireland—the very core of English rule—and, in the eyes of the Irish chiefs and people, the symbol of alien domination. In one sense its history is not eventful since it never suffered siege or violent capture, though it was seized, bloodlessly, more than once, notably at the Restoration and the coming of William III. As a collection of buildings, its history is one of accident and decay, neglect, reparation and rebuilding.

Bedford Tower dominates the upper yard, flanked by two baroque arches bearing statues of Fortitude and Justice by Van Nost—the Castle authorities are said to have pierced holes in Justice's scales for when it rained they would tip

45. Statue of Mars on Castle gateway
46. Dublin Castle in Brooking's Map, *1728*

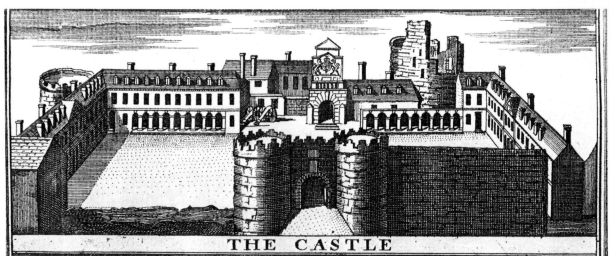

THE CASTLE

off balance, inciting sardonic comments on 'British justice' from the Dublin populace. The Genealogical Museum (open 10–1 and 2.30–4, Monday to Friday) is situated in the room whence the Irish Crown Jewels were stolen at the time of Edward VII's state visit in 1907. The cupola sits on one of the round towers of the old north gate of the castle. Bedford Tower dates from *c.* 1740, and is first seen on Joseph Tudor's engraving of 1753. The portico *in antis* forms a loggia where the band used to play for military parades in the yard below. A top storey has been added here as well as to all the other buildings in the Upper Castle Yard. The Viceroy's aides de camp and master of ceremonies lived here.

The State Apartments, which are on view to the public, are opposite the Bedford Tower. They were the Viceroy's winter quarters, where he held his levées and entertainments. A large ball was held on St. Patrick's Day and on the King's Birthday in St. Patrick's Hall, the most splendid ballroom in Dublin. It is used today for Government entertaining and for the

47. Cupola, upper yard
48. Great Court Yard, Dublin Castle *by James Malton, 1790. St. Werburgh's spire was soon to be taken down*

49. St. Patrick's Hall, Dublin Castle

48

49

ceremony of installing the President. The ceiling was painted in 1778 by Vincent Waldré, who was brought to Ireland by the Marquess of Buckingham when Viceroy, for whom he had worked at Stowe. The three huge ceiling panels represent St. Patrick converting the Druids, George III supported by Justice and Liberty (an allegorical expression of the flourishing state of the country) and Henry II receiving the submission of the Irish chiefs. The walls are hung with the arms and insignia of the Knights of St. Patrick (K.P.), a now obsolete Order which was the Irish equivalent of the Garter. Lord Buckingham founded the Order and St. Patrick's Hall was used for the installation ceremony. The Throne Room or Battle Axe Hall is white and gold, with one of several modern Donegal carpets designed for the Castle by Raymond McGrath. Some good Dublin plasterwork from Mespil House and Tracton House has found a new home in the rooms off the splendid corridor designed by Pearce. Until the addition of the top storey this was lit from above. Many of these rooms are new, because this part of the Castle suffered from a fire in 1940, and has been restored by Raymond McGrath and Oscar Richardson of the Office of Public Works.

The Chapel Royal is an essay in pointed gothic by Francis Johnston, 1807, built on the site of two earlier chapels. Renamed the Church of the Most Holy Trinity in 1943, it has now become a Catholic church. It was approached from the State Apartments down a battlemented gothic corridor which skirts the south side of the Wardrobe or Record Tower. The coats of arms of the successive Viceroys are carved in panels in the gallery; there proved to be exactly the right number as the arms of the last Viceroy fill the last panel. The Chapel is richly decorated and between carvings and figures in the stained glass windows the

concourse includes St. Patrick, Brian Boru, the Virgin Mary, Dean Swift, St. Peter, Christ, Pilate and the Evangelists. The elaborate plaster fan tracery was the work of George Stapleton, son of Michael, in imitation of the stone vaulting in a medieval church. The woodwork was carved by Richard Stewart and the stonework by Edward Smyth.

The lower yard has been greatly

50. Waldré's sketch for the ceiling in St. Patrick's Hall (Courtesy of the Royal Dublin Society)

51. *The Throne Room, Dublin Castle*

52. *Painting and plasterwork in the Throne Room*

53. *The Supper Room, Dublin Castle*

spoiled by the new offices built on the site of a harmless stable block which used to house the National Museum's collection of carriages.

54. ABOVE *The Chapel Royal, Dublin Castle, now the Church of the Most Holy Trinity*

55. RIGHT ABOVE *South front Dublin Castle*

The Fountain, James's Street

The Fountain, James's Street, was designed by Francis Sandys and used to be crowned with a circular knob. There is a sundial near the top on each face of the four-sided obelisk.

56. Sundial, James's Street

The Four Courts

The Courts of Law are accommodated in James Gandon's second great building on the north bank of the Liffey after the Custom House, begun in 1786. Thomas Cooley's Public Record Offices, begun ten years earlier, are incorporated in the western range, but little of this is visible except in the window casings of the extreme western wall. The great granite complex was bombarded and burnt during the Civil War by Free State troops and battle scars can be seen on the Portland stone portico. It was re-built more or less the same, but the interior which can be seen in Gandon's section is lost forever, as are the documents in the Public Record Office, full to overflowing with papers especially brought in for safe-keeping, which went up in smoke at the same time. The east and west ranges were shortened by one bay and are nearly flush with the arcaded masonry screens. These centre on triumphal arches, bearing emblems of Justice and Law, and surmounted by balls where formerly there had been crowns. Edward Smyth carved these embellishments and also provided the five statues on the central block representing Wisdom, Justice, Moses, Mercy and Authority. Smyth also decorated the interior of the central rotunda with immense plaster figures and it had a coffered dome with a central opening to the room above. This upper rotunda, which has the finest views in Dublin, was first intended as a library, then for storing records, and probably on account of its altitude has never found a use.

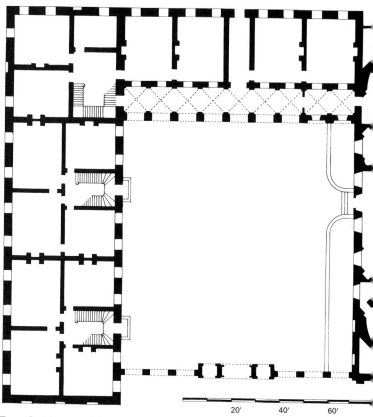

Four Courts, ground floor

20' 40' 60'

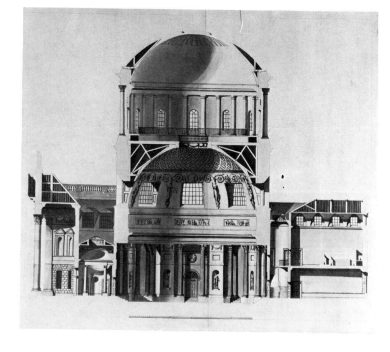

57. RIGHT *Gandon's section of the Four Courts*
58. CENTRE *Trophies by Edward Smyth*
59. FAR RIGHT *Statue representing Punishment, by Edward Smyth*

54

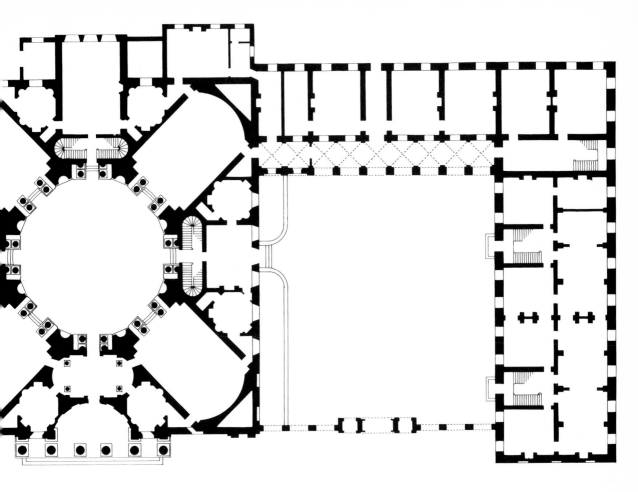

The General Post Office, Lower O'Connell Street

Francis Johnston's monumental Post Office was completed in 1818. It was recently cleaned and, like so many other of the great public buildings in the city today, it smiles where once it frowned. The massive granite building with its Greek Revival portico is a part of Irish history, for it was seized by Pearse and Connolly at the Easter Uprising of 1916, and the Proclamation declaring an Irish Republic was issued from here. In the subsequent fighting the building was gutted, but it has been rebuilt and the statue of Cuchulain within symbolises the martyrdom of those who gave their lives for their ideals.

The Nelson Pillar was six years older than the Post Office (and fifty years older than the one in Trafalgar Square). It was blown up in 1966, the fiftieth anniversary of the Easter Rising, and a bed of forget-me-nots was thoughtfully planted where it stood.

60. General Post Office façade

61. Cuchulain statue, G.P.O.

Green Street Courthouse

The Green Street Courthouse, behind the Four Courts, is still in use; it was designed by Richard Johnston, the architect of the Gate Theatre, in 1792.

62. Green Street Courthouse

Guinness's Brewery, St. James's Gate

Guinness's Brewery is perhaps the largest industry in Dublin, producing two million barrels of stout a year as well as other types of beer. Arthur Guinness purchased an existing brewery in 1759, when there were 300 other brewers in the city—in those days most publicans made their own brew. Today 'Uncle Arthur', as the firm is affectionately called, is the only brewery in Dublin, and it extends over 64 acres on either side of St. James's Gate, filling the air with delicious smells. Visitors are welcome to the Visit Centre, Crane Street (off Thomas Street), where they are shown a film of the brewing process and given a free sample of the product. It is open from 10 a.m.–3 p.m., except Saturdays, Sundays and Bank Holidays.

The cone-shaped tower with St. Patrick on its weather vane was a windmill in the eighteenth century and is a landmark on many an old painting of the city. It has lost its wings, but the

63. LEFT *Front gate,*
Guinness's Brewery

64. *Gateway to*
Brewery which
formerly led to a
military infirmary

top still revolves; it was commandeered for use as a machine-gun post in the Troubles. The main entrance, bearing the date of the founding of the business and the present date, has become a symbol of the firm. More elegant still is the archway across the street which once led to a military infirmary, and is embellished with colourful military trophies. There is also a Brewery Museum on Watling Street which the curator will show to visitors by appointment.

Harcourt Street Station

The terminus of the old Dublin and
South-Eastern Railway in Harcourt
Street is no longer open to traffic but
survives as offices. It was designed by
George Wilkinson in 1859 to serve the
line to Bray and Wexford. It ranks with
the Broadstone as the noblest of
Dublin's many railway stations, and has
none of the Italianate frivolity of
Kingsbridge or Amiens Street although
it was built well into the reign of
Victoria.

65. Harcourt Street Station

Sean Heuston (*formerly* Kingsbridge) Station

Across the Liffey from the main
entrance to the Phoenix Park there is a
handsome Victorian railway station,
built to look like a country house,
which serves the cities of Cork and
Limerick. It was the terminus of the
Great Southern and Western Railway,
and was built in 1845 by Sancton
Wood, the English railway architect.
On winning the architectural
competition instituted by the Great
Southern and Western Railway
Company, for Kingsbridge, as it was
then known, he became architect to the
company; the stations he built down the
line are, however, in the gothic style.

66. Kingsbridge Station

Kilmainham Gaol

Kilmainham Gaol has been restored by a voluntary committee and was rescued from advanced decay at the eleventh hour. It is open to the public on Sunday afternoons. The prison was completed in 1796 to the designs of Sir John Traile, architect of the Marshalsea, canal engineer, and High Sheriff of Co. Dublin. It served Dublin County while Newgate Gaol (designed by Thomas Cooley in 1773) served the city. Executions were carried out in front of the prison, where the doorway with its maggot-like rustication is surmounted by five chained serpents known as 'the Five Devils of Kilmainham'.

67. Interior,
Kilmainham Gaol

68. Doorway,
Kilmainham Gaol

The King's Inns, Henrietta Street

The first stone of the Dublin equivalent of the London Inns of Court was laid in 1795. The design of the original building was James Gandon's, but following a dispute with Lord Chancellor Redesdale, Gandon resigned and left his pupil and partner, Henry Aaron Baker, in charge. On the Henrietta Street side the building closes off the street at a surprising angle, and there is a curved screen pierced by a triumphal arch bearing the Royal Arms. To the left is the Registry of Deeds, and opposite the great Dining Hall, the only one of Gandon's major interiors to survive unscathed. The front facing across to the Broadstone Station is surmounted by a cupola, added by Francis Johnston to Gandon's design in 1816. This façade was lengthened by three bays at either side in the middle of the last century, tactfully done to echo Gandon's perennial dislike of windows. The carved ornament is by Edward Smyth.

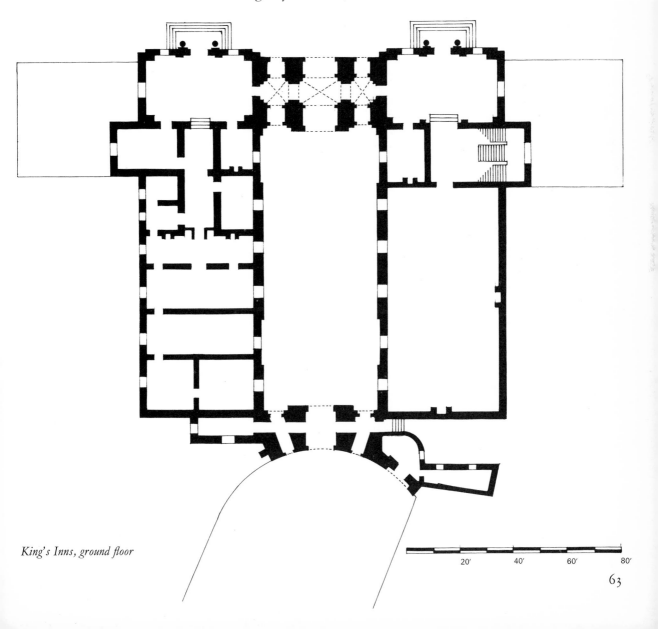

King's Inns, ground floor

20'   40'   60'   80'

69. Garden front,
King's Inns

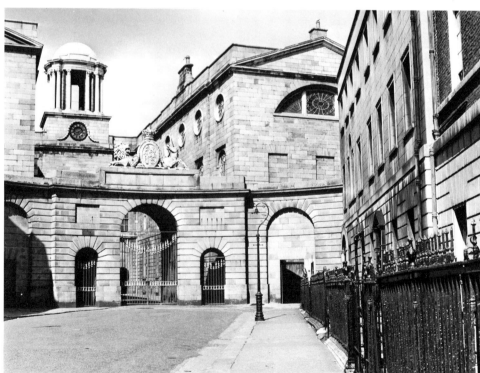

70. Henrietta Street
side of King's Inns

71. Entrance hall,
King's Inns

72. Dining Hall
fireplace

65

73. Dining Hall, King's Inns

Marsh's Library, St. Patrick's Close

Archbishop Marsh's library is built on part of the grounds of the former Palace of St. Sepulchre, now a Police Barracks. It was built of brick in 1703 to the designs of Sir William Robinson, the architect of the Royal Hospital,

Kilmainham. The side opposite St. Patrick's Cathedral was faced in stone at the time of Sir Benjamin Guinness's restoration of the cathedral in the 1860s, and the gothic entrance and battlements date from this period. The brick appears

74. Marsh's Library entrance

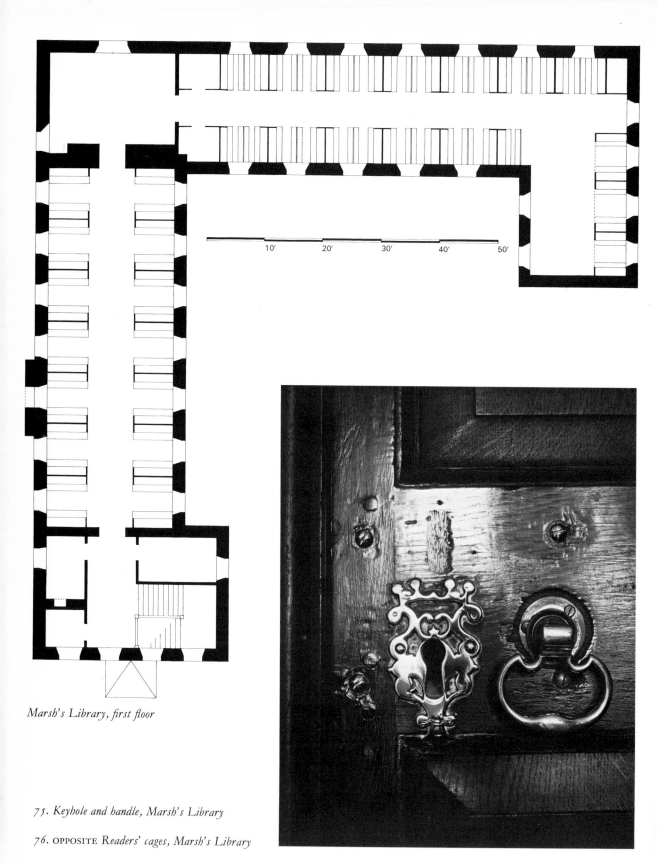

Marsh's Library, first floor

75. Keyhole and handle, Marsh's Library

76. OPPOSITE Readers' cages, Marsh's Library

to have been replaced also, as it has a hard Victorian appearance.

The interior has remained intact, and the dark oak bookcases with their quaintly carved and lettered gables, each topped by a mitre, are unaltered. The decorative cages, where readers were locked in to prevent pilfering, can still be seen.

Marsh's Library was the only free public library in Dublin until 1820

when the Royal Dublin Society opened its doors to one and all. The library of Stillingfleet, Bishop of Worcester, comprising 9,500 volumes, forms the basis of the collection; this is housed in the first gallery, as placed by Marsh himself. Visiting hours are from 2–4 p.m. on Mondays; 10.30 a.m.–12.30 p.m. and 2–4 p.m. on Wednesdays, Thursdays and Fridays; 10.30 a.m.–12.30 p.m. on Saturdays.

The Newcomen Bank, Castle Street

The Newcomen Bank faces the west front of the City Hall, and is now used as offices by Dublin Corporation. It was designed in 1781 by Thomas Ivory as a tall narrow house of three bays on each front, faced in Portland stone, and adorned with adamesque swags. In 1858 it was doubled in size and a large porch was clamped on to join the new to the old. The plan of the old half is particularly ingenious, with a grand oval staircase leading to a vast oval room, once the office of Sir William Gleadowe Newcomen, M.P., the banker for whom it was built.

Newcomen Bank, upper floor

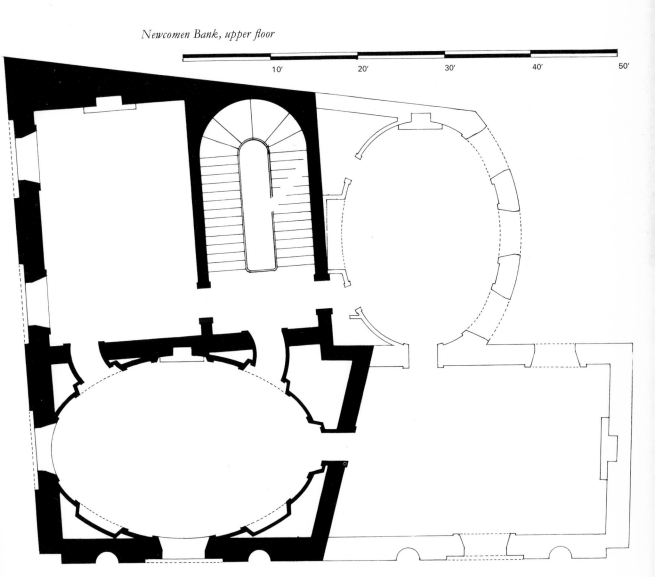

10' 20' 30' 40' 50'

78. *The Newcomen Bank, now offices of the Department of Health. A Victorian porch on the east front links the original building on the left to its replica*

79. *Newcomen Bank: the main entrance on Castle Street*

The Parliament House – *now the Bank of Ireland*

Sir Edward Lovett Pearce designed the monumental Parliament House to house the House of Commons and the House of Lords; it faces Trinity College across College Green and is widely considered to be the most important building in Dublin. 'Speaker' William Conolly, for whom Pearce had also worked at Castletown, Co. Kildare, was present at the laying of the foundation stone in 1729, a few months before he died. A colonnaded entrance court gave into the Court of Requests, then to a lobby, and thence to the great octagonal Commons chamber, directly on axis to the front portico. Light came from a vast Venetian window and there were smaller windows high up beneath the dome. The benches were upholstered in

green. A giant colonnade surrounded the room behind which there was a gallery; visitors sat between the great Doric columns when they came to debates, and there was room for seven hundred spectators.

Neither the date nor place of Pearce's birth is known, but he is thought to have been born in Ireland in 1699; if so he was only thirty years old when he designed his masterpiece. He had travelled in Italy and his annotated copy of Palladio's *Quattro Libri* is in Worcester College, Oxford. He became Surveyor General of Ireland in 1730 on the death of Thomas Burgh, but only lived to enjoy the post for three years.

The House of Lords has survived as designed by Pearce, still hung with tapestries woven for the room by 'Jan van Beaver, ye famous tapestry weaver' and lit by a glass chandelier, most likely made in Dublin, not Waterford. Thomas Oldham was paid £10 11s 0d

80. Early edition of James Malton's view of Parliament House, showing pigs being driven past, 1790. The pigs were later erased. See *Introduction p. 11*

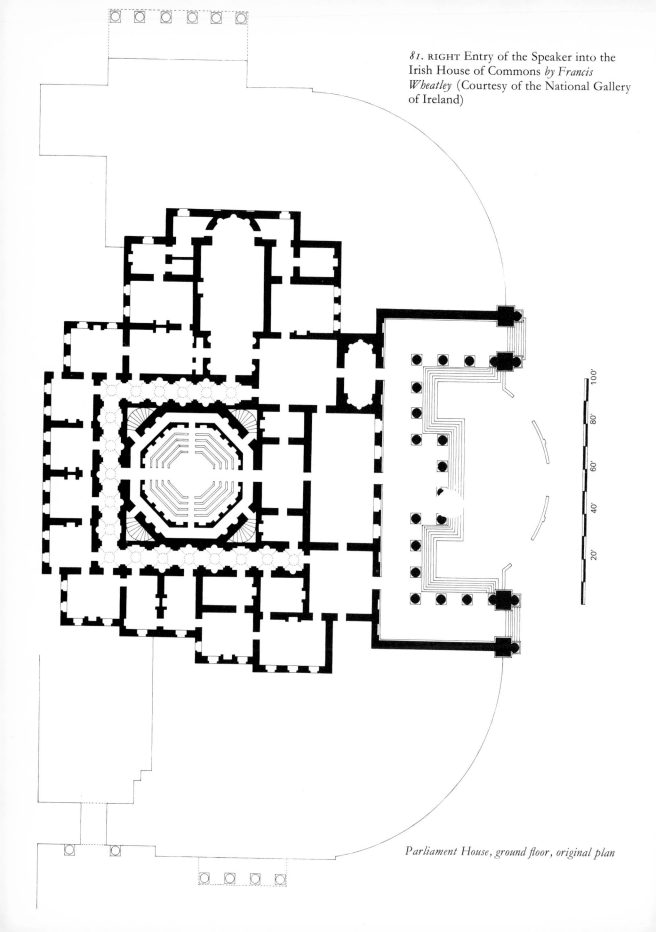

81. RIGHT Entry of the Speaker into the
Irish House of Commons *by Francis
Wheatley* (Courtesy of the National Gallery
of Ireland)

100'

80'

60'

40'

20'

Parliament House, ground floor, original plan

82. BELOW *Part of the tapestry by Jan van Beaver can be seen here above the mantelpiece in the House of Lords*

for finishing the Chimney Piece of the House of Lords 'according to the Designs of Inigo Jones'. It can be visited during banking hours.

The House of Lords gained an entrance of its own in 1785, when the Corinthian portico fronting on Westmorland Street was begun. Originally designed as a six-columned Ionic portico in 1782, Gandon's change of conception was in deference to Pearce's Ionic south front. When questioned as to the propriety of introducing a different style to the building, the architect replied that he was 'working to the Order of the House of Lords'.

The House of Lords portico was linked to the main front of the Parliament House by a curved screen wall, plain except for niches, designed by Gandon at the same time. He also commissioned three statues by Edward Smyth, representing Wisdom, Justice and Liberty. Robert Parke was the architect responsible for balancing this curved screen when the Commons needed more space and it was decided to expand to the west. He designed the portico on Foster Place in 1792, and linked it to Pearce's south front with an open curved colonnade making a quarter circle. This addition was not unanimously praised. First of all it did not match Gandon's screen wall to the east, and worse still, it threatened the dominance of Pearce's colonnaded forecourt.

The Act of Union occurred at an opportune moment for the inadequately housed Bank of Ireland, and the bank purchased the building in 1803 for £40,000. The Building Committee was unanimous in recommending the abolition of Parke's open colonnade, showing a sensitivity not always found in financial circles. In the interests of symmetry, the inner curved wall of Parke's colonnade was advanced by twelve feet to match Gandon's on the east, and its free-standing columns

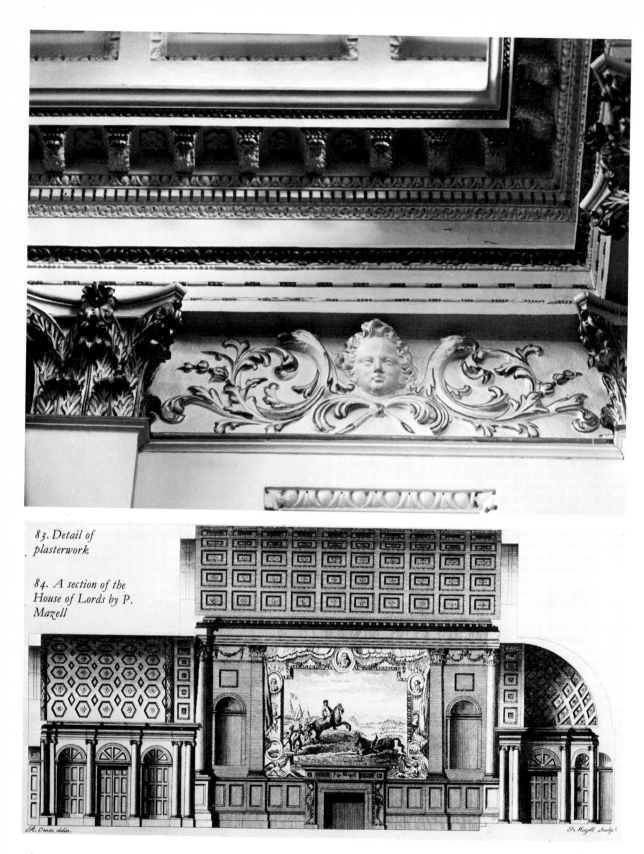

83. Detail of
plasterwork

84. A section of the
House of Lords by P.
Mazell

85. ABOVE *Military trophies carved by Thomas Kirk*
86. *Francis Johnston's gate, Foster Place*

became three-quarter columns. At the same time matching pilasters were added to Gandon's screen wall to balance the whole.

The cash office occupies the space where the Court of Requests once stood and is the work of Francis Johnston, whose strength of design is a good match for that of Pearce nearly a hundred years before. Johnston also designed the monumental arch or guard room that closes Foster Place, surmounted by the military trophies carved by Thomas Kirk. A building conceived at so many different dates by different hands might easily have lost its impact; the Parliament House is a monument to their good taste.

The Phoenix Park

The Phoenix Park which lies at the western end of the city on the north bank of the Liffey is 1,752 acres in extent, and larger than any other city park. As you enter from Park Gate, the *Wellington Testimonial* is on your left. This great obelisk, brilliantly sited so as to be visible from far down the Dublin quays, was designed by Robert Smirke and built with £26,000 subscribed after Waterloo. On your right, past the *People's Garden*, can be seen Gandon's handsome Military Infirmary, now the Army *G.H.Q.* The *Dublin Zoo*, where lions were first bred in captivity, is also near the main entrance to the Park.

Football, cricket and polo grounds are soon in view; early in the morning strings of racehorses can be seen, each with a halo of mist, at exercise on the 'fifteen acres' where there are turf dust gallops. As this is the widest open space in the park, stretching to at least 100 acres, the name is misleading.

Carved out of the Park are the grounds of the President's house, formerly the Viceregal Lodge, now known as *Aras an Uachtarain*; the *American Embassy* and the former *Papal Nuncio's Residence* (once the Chief Secretary and Under Secretary's Lodges). A Phoenix rising from flames surmounts a column which stands beside the great central drive by the entrance to Aras an Uachtarain. Lord Chesterfield, when Viceroy (1745), erected it in the middle of the road, but it was moved to one side when motor racing took place in the Park. The Phoenix Column can be seen on an old printed linen or 'toile', commemorating an actual event – the Provincial Review (of the Province of Leinster, 1782) of the Irish Volunteers. Lord Charlemont, with bared head, is

87. The Wellington Testimonial, Phoenix Park
88. RIGHT Chapel in the grounds of the former Hibernian Military School, Phoenix Park

89. Army G.H.Q.

90. Phoenix Column

taking the parade, and some of the troops are actively trying to keep the spectators in their place (see endpapers).

Aras an Uachtarain was built by the Park Ranger, Nathaniel Clements (himself an amateur architect), in 1751, and became the official residence of the Viceroy a few years later. Milton's *Views of Seats* contains an engraving of the house in 1783, when it was a red brick building with curved sweeps and wings. In 1816 Francis Johnston added the south portico and greatly enlarged the house, plastering over the red brick but leaving the curved curtain walls and much of the interior as they were.

The house contains some exceptionally fine plasterwork; the 'Aesop' ceiling was always here, but the finest ceiling from Mespil House, representing the 'Four Elements', was recently imported, as were copies of the Francini plasterwork at Riverstown, Co. Cork. The Riverstown ceiling in the saloon represents 'Time rescuing Truth from the assaults of Discord and Envy' and there are eight wall panels containing classical figures.

Second only to the Italian Embassy in elegance, the United States Embassy

residence occupies the former Chief Secretary's Lodge of the British administration. Situated opposite the President's house, and set in its own grounds, the house faces across the racehorse gallops to the Dublin mountains. It was enlarged for Sir John Blacquiere *c.* 1775. The garden front has a series of arched windows, flanked by two bays. The extensive walled gardens are at their best in May.

91. FAR LEFT ABOVE *Entrance front, Aras an Uachtarain*
92. FAR LEFT *Entrance hall, Aras an Uachtarain*
93. ABOVE *The Viceregal Lodge, an engraving in Milton's* View of Seats, *1783*
94. LEFT *Dining room, Aras an Uachtarain*

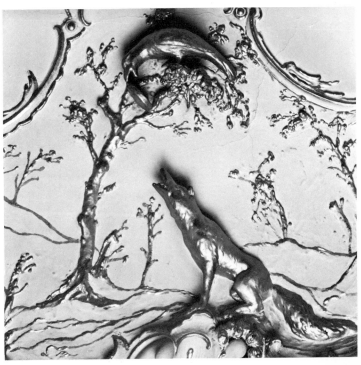

95. *Drawing room, Aras an Uachtarain*

96. *Aesop ceiling, detail of fox*
97. *'Four Elements' ceiling, Jupiter*

98. United States Embassy
99. United States Embassy interior

Portobello House

The former Grand Canal Hotel at Portobello was built in 1807 by the canal 'company's architect and assistant engineer, Mr. Colbourne'. It served for many years as a nursing home. The harbour it overlooked, resort of swans, has recently been filled in but the old hotel has been beautifully restored by John Costello with proper windows and the cupola replaced. In the heyday of the canal age, the Portobello Hotel was first in a chain of hotels stretching to the Shannon that were operated by the Grand Canal Company. Now closed to commercial traffic, the canal is becoming increasingly used by pleasure craft.

100. Huband Bridge on the Grand Canal

The Rotunda Hospital

Dr. Bartholomew Mosse devoted his life to lowering the birth mortality rate among the poor of Dublin. He established his Lying-in Hospital as a charity, financed out of his own pocket and by public subscription, lotteries and grants from Parliament. Richard Castle was the architect, but as he died the year building commenced, John Ensor, his pupil and assistant, found himself in charge of the work. The labour wards as laid out for Dr. Mosse are still in use, although the gilded Ball and Cradle weathervane that was on the cupola in 1754 is no longer in place, having been pronounced unsafe twenty years later. The gardens, laid out behind the hospital and used by it for raising money in imitation of Vauxhall in London, have unfortunately since been built over.

Rotunda Hospital, ground floor plan, since altered by modern additions

Originally four curved sweeps framed the building, two on either front. Its chief beauty is the little Church of Ireland chapel above the front hall, which has elaborate contemporary plasterwork by Bartholomew Cramillion with allegories related to the function of the hospital. Dr. Mosse died in 1759, and as a result the ceiling, which was to have been adorned with a painting of the Nativity by Cipriani, was left plain. Such elaborate and costly decoration might seem out of place in a charity hospital where funds were ever in short supply, but it served as a draw for fashionable society. A good tear-wringing sermon could raise £1,000 in one morning, provided the right people were there to open their purses.

Small parties are allowed to visit the chapel by applying to the porter at the

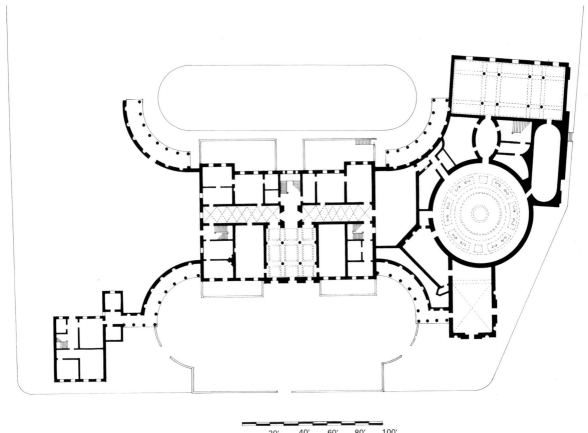

20'   40'   60'   80'   100'

102. Rotunda
Hospital

103. The Rotunda as
designed by Ensor

front desk. The decoration has the following meaning:

Above the Altar: The Lamb of God on a book with seven seals (Revelation V, v. 1), and the figure of Charity, as a mother with children.
In the corresponding position on the right wall: Hope, with her anchor.
On the left wall: Faith blindfold, with cross, Bible and plummet of righteousness, in contrast to the coiled serpent. Underfoot she crushes a fox. The fox is said to spoil vines (Song of Solomon II. v. 15), which here festoon the corners and represent the children (Psalm CXXVIII. v. 3).
In the recess above the organ: One angel blows a trumpet for the Last Judgement, and another points to the Ten Commandments.

On the ceiling: Four scrolls display texts:
1 Above the pulpit: 'The children are come to the birth, and there is not strength to bring forth' (Isaiah XXXVII. v. 3).
2 Above the lectern: 'Kings shall be thy nursing fathers, and their queens thy nursing mothers' (Isaiah XLIX. v. 23).
3 Above the font: 'That our sons may grow up as the young plants, and that our daughters may be as the polished corners of the temple' (Psalm CXLIV. v. 12).
4 Also: 'Out of the mouths of babes and sucklings thou hast perfected praise' (St. Matthew XXI. v. 16).

104. View of the altar

In 1764 John Ensor added a round assembly hall to the east that could be used to earn additional revenue for the hospital, since then known as the Rotunda. It was originally of brick, but Gandon had it plastered to tone in with the stone buildings on either side, and concealed the ungainly conical roof behind a parapet ornamented with neo-classical swags and plaques in Coadestone. In 1784 Richard Johnston, brother of Francis, designed two more assembly rooms, one above the other, now the Gate Theatre and the Pillar Room; they still belong to the hospital.

105 and 106. Plasterwork in Rotunda Chapel

107. *Front hall,
Rotunda Hospital*

108. *Inside the Gate
Theatre*

The Royal Hospital, Kilmainham

In 1680 the Duke of Ormonde laid the first stone of the hospital for old soldiers which, like Wren's Chelsea Hospital, was based on the Invalides in Paris. It is the most important secular building of its period in Ireland, and stands on a commanding site across the Liffey from Phoenix Park. No proper use had been found for the building in recent years and it was closed to the public; however, some restoration work was done on the spire and roof. It is now to be fully restored as a conference centre.

The Surveyor-General, Sir William Robinson, was the architect, although the building is frequently attributed to Wren. It was built in the form of a large square courtyard with limestone arcades for exercise in wet weather, the walls of rubble plastered. The principal front has tall rounded windows facing north, and

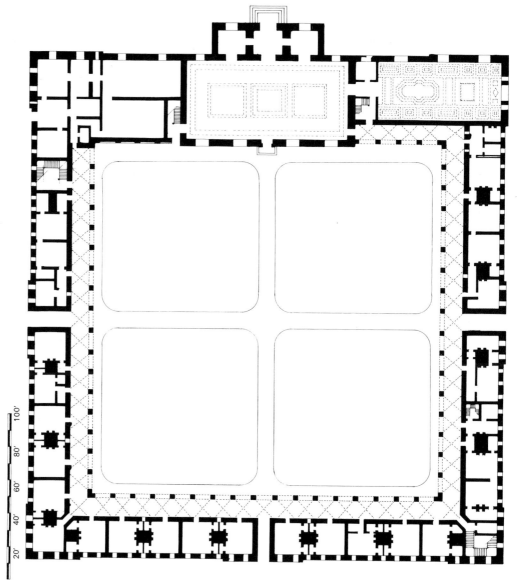

Royal Hospital,
ground floor

92

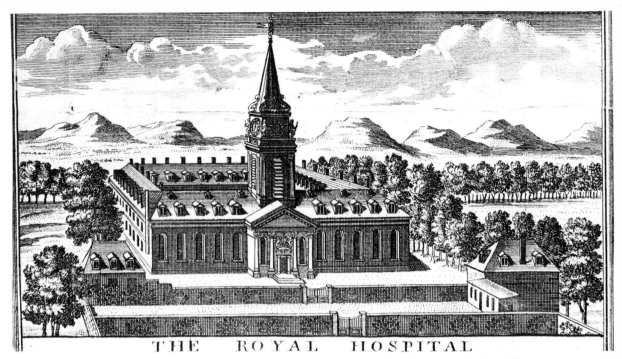

THE ROYAL HOSPITAL

109. The Royal Hospital, from Brooking's
Map of Dublin, *1728*
110. East front, Royal Hospital

contains the Chapel, Hall and
Governor's apartments; the military
Commander-in-Chief in Ireland
customarily held this position. The arms
of Ormonde in carved stone surmount
the pediment in the centre of this front,
beneath the tower and spire that were
completed in 1701. In the chapel is a
papier-mâché replica, erected in 1902, of
the great Carolean plaster ceiling.
Evidently in the original the
enrichments were mounted on oak
twigs which, after two hundred years,
began to rot and snap so that those at
worship found themselves rewarded
unexpectedly from above. The carved
oak woodwork and altar are by James
Tabary, a Huguenot. During the short
reign of James II the 'service of the
Church of Rome' was celebrated here.
The east window has medieval tracery
said to have come from the old Priory
of the Knights Hospitallers which had
occupied this site. Malton's view shows

111. Restoration work in progress

112. Royal Hospital, aerial view

113. Chapel ceiling

The Four Courts

The Parliament House, now the Bank of Ireland. The
tapestry is by Jan van Beaver.

the glazing of the chapel windows facing north, before they were given their present form in the last century. The last service to be held here was in 1927.

The hall ceiling was 'in a very massive and heavy style, divided into three compartments, the centre of which is occupied by the dial of a clock, about 10 feet in diameter'. This was replaced in the nineteenth century by a neo-Tudor ceiling. The walls of the hall were wainscotted in oak, whereon were displayed swords and guns as in an armoury. Above, there hung twenty-two full-length portraits of Kings, Queens, Viceroys and Lords Justice, the latest dated 1737. A gallery ran along the south side of the hall, leading from the apartments of the Governor to his elevated pew at the back of the chapel, where he sat beneath a carved canopy. This gallery was 'supported by brackets of carved oak, representing different figures, as large as life.'

To the north there is a formal garden, closed by the now ruinous aide de camp's house; the ghost of the last classical garden in the city. A straight avenue of lime trees leads to the west, where a gothic gateway stands, designed by Francis Johnston. Originally sited beside the Liffey at Bloody Bridge, with the coming of the railway in 1846 this gateway was taken down stone by stone for re-erection on its present site. It was then discovered that the architect had inserted his own coat of arms, concealed from view behind a piece of wood painted to look like stone. Johnston evidently intended that when the wood decayed his arms would be revealed for ever more, an innocent conceit thwarted by the moving of the gate, a circumstance he could hardly have foreseen.

114. *Wood carving by James Tabary*
115. *Francis Johnston's gateway, Royal Hospital, Kilmainham*

St. Patrick's Hospital, Bow Lane

St. Patrick's, generally known as Swift's Hospital because it was built with money bequeathed by the Dean for that purpose, was designed in 1749 by George Semple. The wings were added by Thomas Cooley in 1778. There is a good collection of Swiftiana in the hospital and the original builders' account book and designs for the building are also preserved here.

116. St. Patrick's Hospital

Sir Patrick Dun's Hospital, Artichoke Road

Henry Aaron Baker, the pupil of
Gandon, designed Sir Patrick Dun's
Hospital and building began in 1803.
One wing was for male patients and the
other for females. The main front faces
north and is rather bleak; it would be
greatly improved if the Georgian
glazing could be replaced. The interior
retains some handsome features.

*117. Sir Patrick
Dun's Hospital*

*118. Woodwork in
Sir Patrick Dun's
Hospital*

Tailors Hall, Back Lane

The headquarters of the Guild of Tailors dates from 1706 and, as would be expected in a building of this date, is of brick. It stands in Back Lane, near Christ Church Cathedral, and the hall was customarily available for hire. In 1792 it achieved lasting fame by being let to the Catholic Committee of the United Irishmen, whose secretary was the Protestant patriot Wolfe Tone. Representatives of the Roman Catholic communities all over Ireland held formal discussions here on matters such as Emancipation and the Penal Laws. This historic meeting was nicknamed the Back Lane Parliament. The hall, which came into the possession of Dublin Corporation at the dissolution of the guilds in 1830, was allowed to fall into such a state of disrepair that it was closed as a dangerous building in 1960. The last tenants were the Legion of Mary. In 1965, as a result of a public meeting in Dublin, a committee was formed for the purpose of raising funds

119. Mantelpiece in Tailors Hall, the gift of the wardens, Neary, Bell and Craigg

120. Tailors Hall during restoration

*121. Gateway to
Tailors Hall*

to save the hall, and it has been
restored by Mr. Austin Dunphy.

The front door, dated 1770, leads
into a narrow entrance hall and thence
to the staircase with its barley-sugar
banisters. The hall is lit by tall round-
headed windows; at one end there are
panels with the names of the successive
masters of the guild, and at the other a
minstrels' gallery. The narrow cornice is
a copy in plaster of the original one
which was of timber, part of which was
found beneath later work. The mantel is
inscribed 'The gift of Christopher
Neary, master; Alexander Bell and
Hugh Craigg, wardens, 1784'.

Trinity College

Trinity College was founded in the reign of Queen Elizabeth, in 1592, in order to 'civilise' the Irish and put an end to their studying on the Continent 'whereby they have been infected with Popery . . .'. Although most of the students, and indeed faculty, have been Catholic for as long as anyone can remember, Trinity is still considered a Protestant stronghold, and until recently the Catholic Archbishop of Dublin preached against it with great eloquence in his Lenten Pastoral.

None of the college buildings dates from before 1700. The 'Rubrics' which were given Dutch gables in the 1890s in place of their dormer windows, are the oldest buildings in college, and are all that is left of the red brick Library Square. The fourth side was taken up by the great Library, begun in 1712 to the designs of Thomas Burgh. The stone in the upper part of the building was a pale sandstone, making a pleasant

122. Trinity College

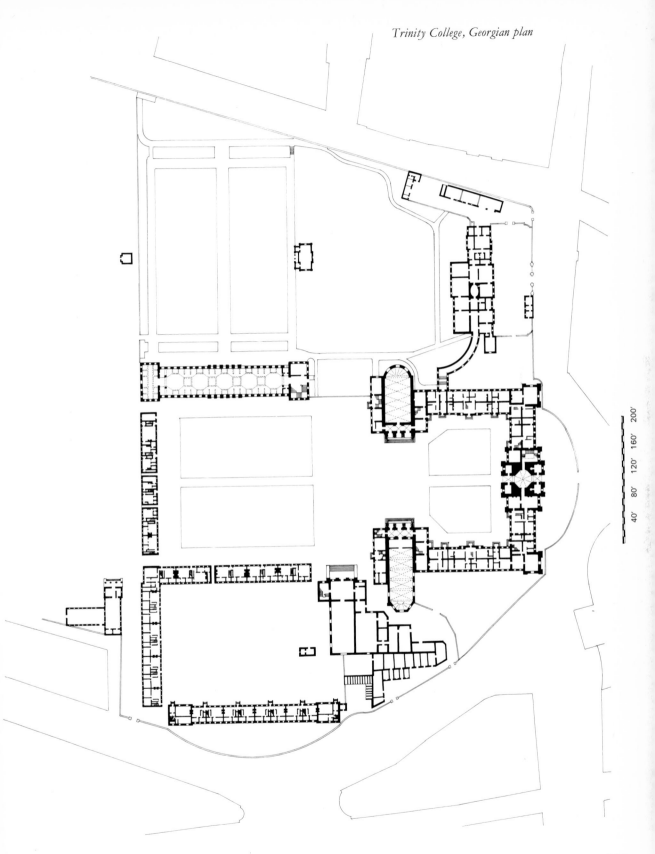

40' 80' 120' 160' 200'

contrast with the dark limestone arcades. The sandstone must have been of poor quality, as the upper floors have since been refaced in granite. Another alteration in the nineteenth century was the removal of the original compartmented plaster ceiling in the Long Room, and its replacement with a timber barrel vault, which sucks out the light. Even so it is one of the great sights of Dublin. Among the treasures on public display here are the Book of Kells, Brian Boru's Harp, and Roubiliac's bust of Swift. The staircase leading up to the Library was designed by Castle. His decorators transcribed literally into plaster the alternate designs that they were given.

The next oldest building in College is the Printing House, designed by Castle in 1734. Its temple-form portico was

123. Trinity College, Library door
124. BELOW *The Library*
125. RIGHT *The Long Room*

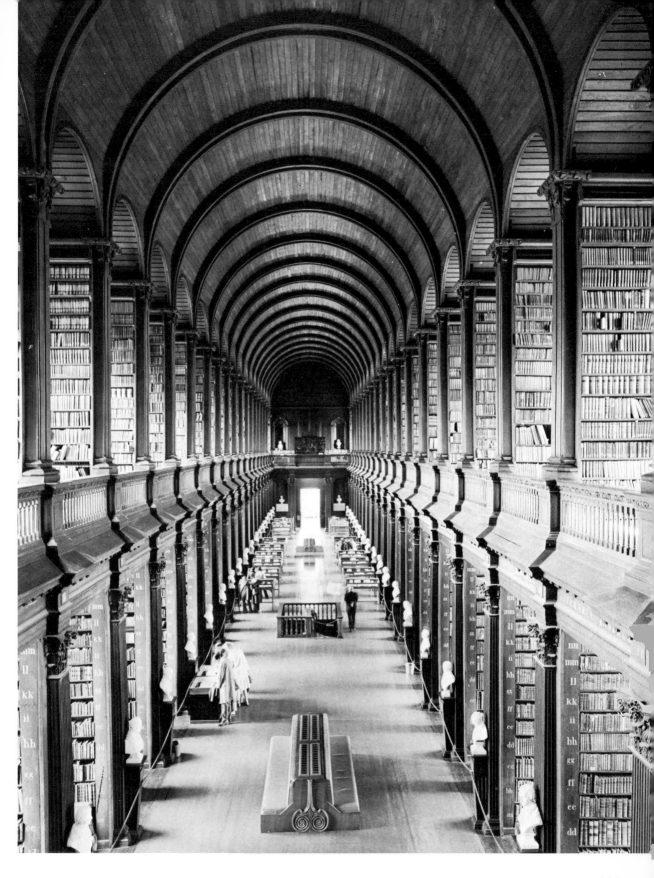

used as an imprint on the title page of College publications. Among these were the large illustrated volumes on Irish architecture produced by the Georgian Society from 1908. Printing was being done in College as early as 1602, when the New Testament in Irish was published here.

Richard Castle was also the architect responsible for the Dining Hall, although he ran into trouble over the construction and it had to be rebuilt. The black marble mantel he designed for the great hall is now in the Common Room, over the front hall, and the mantel in hall today was supplied by George Darley in 1765. Castle's magnificent Bell Tower of 1740 was, according to Dr. McParland, deemed unsafe for the ringing of the bell in 1791. The same authority suggests that the rebuilding of the west front was delayed until Castle's death in 1751, so there would be no obligation to use the plan that he had prepared for it.

126. Printing House, Trinity College

127. Dining Hall, Trinity College

128. Portrait of Frederick, Prince of Wales hangs in the Dining Hall

The west front was fifty years old when it was replaced with the existing Palladian frontage on College Green in 1752. The old front had been of brick with primitive Dutch gables at either end and a narrow central pediment. This design was echoed in the general massing of the new front, begun in the year after Castle's death. The foundations of the projected central dome can be seen at the entrance to College. There were to have been cupolas at either end of the façade, and the northern cupola was actually erected but there was a change of plan and dome and cupolas were abandoned. Above the entrance is the Regent House, used for a time as a natural history museum; it is approached by an elegant staircase with a wrought-iron balustrade.

Dr. McParland has recently attributed the west front to the amateur English architect, Theodore Jacobsen, best known for his design of the

129. The Common Room, Trinity College, with the black marble mantel originally designed for the great hall

130. Trinity College west front

131. The Dining Hall mantel

Foundling Hospital in London. Until this discovery Henry Keene and John Sanderson, who received a payment from the College for their plans, had been credited with this important elevation. Sanderson was the executive architect for Jacobsen in the case of the Foundling Hospital and must have collaborated here also.

Sir William Chambers, who never visited Ireland but had a devoted Irish patron in Lord Charlemont, sent over plans for the Chapel and the Theatre or Examination Hall. These were put up by the college architect, Graham Myers; Chambers wrote in 1779: 'If there be any merit in the general intention I may claim some share of it; but the whole detail, on which the

The Custom House

Dublin Castle

*132. Stairs leading to
Regent House, Trinity
College*

133. Regent House

*134. Mortar board in
stucco, Regent House*

135. Trinity College Chapel

perfection of these works must greatly depend, is none of mine and whatever merit that has is Mr. Myers' who I understand is the operator'. The interior of both buildings has Adamesque plasterwork by Michael Stapleton, and the woodwork in the chapel supporting the curved gallery is particularly well executed.

The Examination Hall contains an elaborate marble monument to the memory of Provost Richard Baldwin, showing him on the point of death, brandishing his will in which he left vast sums to Trinity. It is the work of Christopher Hewetson, an Irish sculptor who worked in Rome. The organ is older than the room.

136. *Examination
Hall, Trinity College*
137. *Monument to
Provost Richard
Baldwin, by Hewetson,
in the Examination
Hall*

The last buildings of the Georgian period in Trinity were the Magnetic Observatory and New Square by Frederick Darley. The little observatory, a Greek pavilion, was taken down recently to make way for the immense new Arts Block which has reared its ugly head at the back of the Provost's House, where there had formerly been lawns and flowering trees. It is in some ways unfortunate for Trinity to be hemmed in by its relatively small site in the centre of Dublin, but there are compensations for the College which it would be the first to acknowledge. Dubliners consider that the few precious green spaces left belong as much to the city as to Trinity, but efforts to persuade the College to site their new building elsewhere met with no success.

*138. The organ,
older than the Examinatio[n]
Hall in which it is housed*

ECCLESIASTICAL BUILDINGS

The Black Church—(*St. Mary's Chapel of Ease*)

The Black Church was designed by John Semple, architect to the Established Church, in 1830 as a chapel of ease to St. Mary's, Mary Street. Semple was not afraid to experiment; his most eccentric creation was Monkstown Church. The Black Church is an elegant example of attenuated gothic, normal enough from outside. Within, the originality of the design becomes apparent; there are neither walls nor ceilings and the interior consists of one vast parabolic vault. The narrow slits of windows appear to lean inwards, giving to some the feeling of being in a tomb, and to others a dizzy sense of intoxication. It is Sir John Betjeman's favourite church in Dublin.

The Black Church was deconsecrated in 1962 and passed into the hands of Dublin Corporation. It is now used for exhibitions and as a headquarters for the traffic wardens.

139. Inside the Black Church   *140. The Black Church*

Christ Church Cathedral

Christ Church Cathedral was built 1176–1230 on the site of the old Norse Cathedral. The Nave collapsed in 1562, and the whole building was in a ruinous state when Mr. Henry Roe, of Roe's Distillery, commissioned George Edmund Street to effect a thorough restoration in 1871. Strongbow's tomb was smashed to pieces by vandals in the sixteenth century, but the Lord Deputy, Sir Philip Sidney, knowing how much it meant to the people of Ireland, had the present effigy transferred here from St. Peter's, Drogheda, to take its place. In the south transept stands the beautiful monument to the 19th Earl of Kildare by Sir Henry Cheere, and in the crypt are two statues, said to be of Charles II and James II, that were removed from the old Tholsel when it was demolished in 1806. James attended Mass in Christ Church during his brief stay in Dublin, and the tabernacle and candlesticks used on this historic occasion are still to be seen, also in the crypt. When the Vikings invaded Ireland in the ninth century they settled upon the little township of Baile-atha-Cliath, 'the town on the ford of hurdles', which they fortified against the Irish. By the eleventh century these Norsemen had adopted Christianity and Dublin was regarded as being in the Province of Canterbury. The Diocese of Dublin transferred its allegiance to the native Church in 1152.

141. Detail of the monument to Robert, 19th Earl of Kildare, by Sir Henry Cheere (1743)

142. Christ Church Cathedral

The Pro-Cathedral, Marlborough Street

Building of the Catholic Pro-Cathedral began in 1815 to the designs of John Sweetman, a much travelled amateur architect who is thought to have been inspired by S. Philippe du Roule in Paris. The dome was an afterthought and is not considered a suitable appendage for a building in the Greek taste. The massive portico is adorned with statues of the Virgin Mary (patron saint), St. Patrick and St. Laurence O'Toole.

143. The Pro-Cathedral

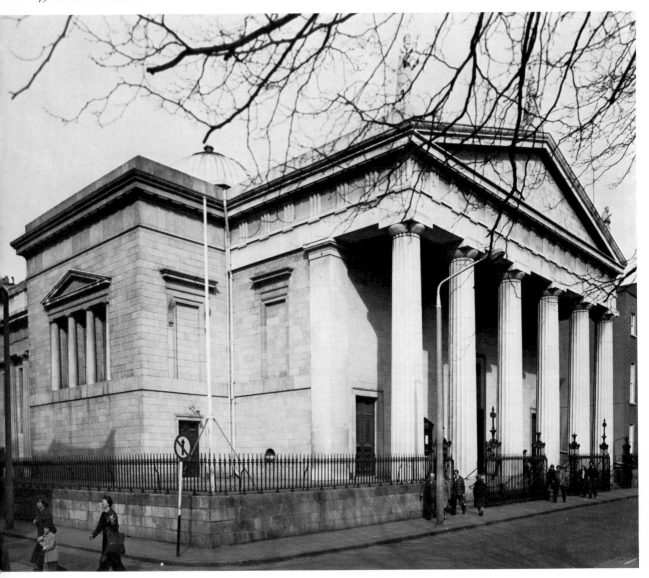

St. Andrew's, Westland Row

The foundation stone of St. Andrew's was laid in 1832 and the church was opened for worship two years later; it is one of the first post-Emancipation Catholic churches in Dublin. Daniel O'Connell, who lived in Merrion Square, as a parishioner was instrumental in the selection of the site, and the architect was James Bolger.

The size of St. Andrew's is not apparent from the street, as the Greek Revival portico is flanked by Parochial houses that were built at the same time. Behind these, the church opens out to its full impressive width. The high altar was imported from Rome, and is surmounted by a sculptural group, representing the Ascension, by John Hogan.

144. St. Andrew's
145. OVERLEAF *Interior of St. Andrew's*

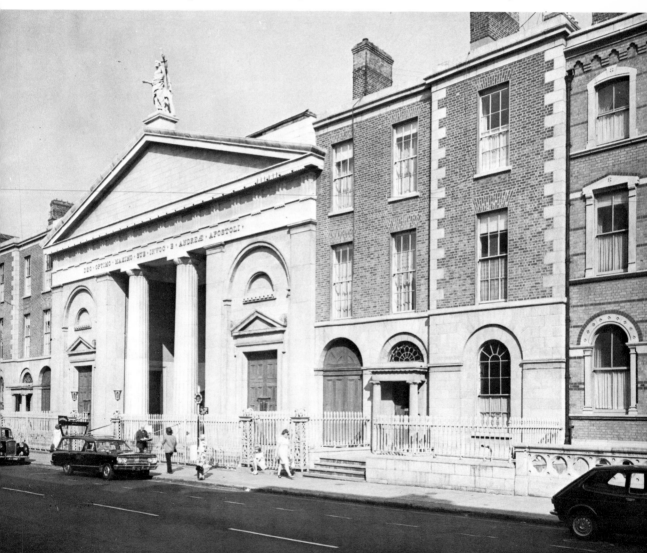

St. Ann's, Dawson Street

Being in a fashionable part of Dublin, St. Ann's has, as would be expected, suffered a great deal from Victorian 'improvements'. The interior has been rendered dark by the intrusion of stained glass. There is an elaborate plaster cornice, and at the east end some gilded plasterwork and woodwork of oak. The gallery is supported by oak pillars, whose capitals have been replaced in the Romanesque style, and there is a good organ case. Lord

146. St. Ann's

Newtown left £13 per annum to be used for distributing bread to the poor, and the shelving put up in 1723 for this purpose is still in use. The Duke of Leinster's canopied chair has been removed long since.

The present front on Dawson Street was designed by Sir Thomas Deane in 1868, but never completed. The original front was an elaborate exercise in the Baroque, designed by Isaac Wills who was the architect of the church in 1720, although the lower half only had in fact been built. There are several good monuments, notably one to Miss Phibbs by Edward Smyth.

147. Interior of St. Ann's

148. Detail of woodwork, St. Ann's

149. The shelving for the bread distributed to the poor, St. Ann's

150. The projected front of St. Ann's on Dawson Street

THE RIGHT HON. THEOPHILUS LORD NEWTOWN OF NEWTOWN BUTLER BEQUEATHᴰ TO THE POOR OF ST. ANNS PARISH FOR EVER THIRTEEN POUNDS PER ANNUM TO BE DISTRIBUTED IN BREAD AT FIVE SHILLINGS EACH WEEK
1723

St. Catherine's Church, Thomas Street

St. Catherine's was designed in 1769 by John Smyth, and the north front facing Thomas Street is the finest classical church façade in Dublin. Having virtually no congregation, the church was closed in 1967 and deconsecrated; the original box pews and the eighteenth-century organ were removed at this time. A voluntary trust has now taken a lease of the building, and has brought back the organ and restored the interior so that St. Catherine's can be used for concerts and meetings. In common with many other Dublin churches, the tower or spire was not finished. The interior has an oak panelled gallery and there is some good plasterwork at the east end; it has been spared Victorian improvements. As one of its projects for European Architectural Heritage Year, 1975, the façade was cleaned and missing stonework replaced by Dublin Corporation, the present owners of St. Catherine's.

151. St. Catherine's north front
152. The organ restored, St. Catherine's

St. George's, Hardwicke Crescent

153. St. George's

It was originally planned to site St. George's Church in the centre of Mountjoy Square, but this scheme was abandoned in favour of siting the church facing a crescent so it is visible down three radial streets. It was designed by Francis Johnston in 1802. The spire, important to the Dublin skyline, is unsafe and may have to be taken down.

The pews and panelling were, until the recent grey and white decoration, a sombre dark brown. The Duke of Wellington was married here; his father-in-law, the Earl of Longford, lived in Rutland (now Parnell) Square.

St. Mark's, Pearse Street

St. Mark's was begun in 1729 and belongs to the family of Protestant churches which includes St. Mary's, St. Werburgh's and St. Catherine's. The interior has arched windows with plain glass, and there is a gallery supported by Corinthian columns. As at St. Catherine's, the tower was never completed. The church retained its box pews until recently. Now de-consecrated, St. Mark's belongs to Trinity College and has been extensively restored; it is used as a hall for various purposes, including theatricals.

154. RIGHT St. Mark's

St. Mary's, Mary Street

St. Mary's, Mary Street, by Thomas Burgh, dates from 1697 and is the only seventeenth-century church in Dublin. Not being in a fashionable quarter today, it has retained its box pews and gallery. The organ is by Renatus Harris and is one of the finest in Dublin.

Unfortunately it is out of action and at present a modern organ in the north gallery is in use. Lord Charlemont was baptised here in 1728 and Wolfe Tone in 1763. John Wesley preached his first sermon in Ireland here in 1747.

155. St. Mary's east window
156. Inside St. Mary's, showing the Renatus Harris organ

SS. Michael & John, Blind Quay

The Church of SS. Michael & John was designed by J. Taylor in 1815, and was the first Catholic church in the city with a bell for summoning the faithful. As this was against the Penal Laws, legal proceedings were instituted to silence the bell. The Parish Priest engaged Daniel O'Connell to defend him, and when this became known no more was heard of the matter.

The granite front, visible from the Quays, has recently been cleaned and the fine gothic detailing is now a pale golden hue. The interior is ornate, with gothic plaster pendants and pilasters, gothic side chapels, and a gothic organ gallery. The confessionals are of unusual design, and there is an elaborate memorial to the Very Rev. Thomas Betagh by Turnerelli.

158. SS. Michael & John

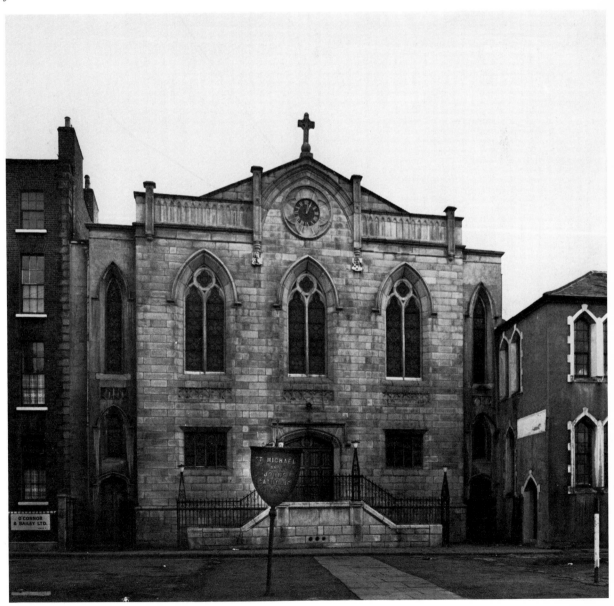

159. Interior of SS. Michael & John

St. Michan's, Church Street

For centuries St. Michan's, named after an early Danish saint, was the only church on the north side of the Liffey, and it was served by the monks of Christ Church Cathedral. The district was exceedingly populous in the late seventeenth century, when the parishes of St. Paul and St. Mary were carved out of it. In 1686 the church was remodelled, but the interior appears to date from *c.* 1810. The organ was erected in 1724 and there is a strong

160. St. Michan's

138

tradition that Handel played it when he was in Dublin for the first performance of the Messiah. The carving of the organ case has been attributed to Cuvilliès.

The high methane content in the air of the vaults beneath the church has resulted in the preservation of the corpses buried there, much visited by the curious. The claims of the 'crusader' to antiquity need not, however, be taken seriously as the vaulting is seventeenth century.

163. Seventeenth-century doorway, St. Michan's

161. Inside St. Michan's

162. Detail of the organ case, St. Michan's

139

St. Patrick's Cathedral

St. Patrick's Cathedral was founded by the first Norman Archbishop of Dublin, but Christ Church managed to retain its Cathedral status also, so that there are two Church of Ireland Cathedrals to this day. The present structure dates from 1220–60, but there was a succession of churches on this site from time immemorial, due to the proximity of a Holy Well associated with St. Patrick. In the sixteenth century the statues of saints and images were all

164. St. Patrick's Cathedral
165. The Boyle tomb, St. Patrick's Cathedral

destroyed under orders from Henry VIII. Cromwell is said to have stabled his horses here. The Lady Chapel was given over to the Huguenots from 1666 to 1816. Cathedral services were held in the Nave, and the north transept was used by the Parish of St. Nicholas Within from the sixteenth century to 1866, when they moved to St. Luke's in the Coombe. The ground plan of 1754 shows how St. Patrick's was divided up until Sir Benjamin Guinness effected his thorough restoration of the fabric in 1864. He removed the screens and wall partitions inside, and replaced the ruinous buttresses and stonework.

Perhaps the most interesting feature is the Boyle monument, the most elaborate seventeenth-century memorial in Ireland, to 'Richard Lord Boyle, Earle of Corke', dated 1631. It was moved from behind the altar, which it overshadowed, to the west end south. The little boy in the centre is Robert Boyle, chemist and philosopher, a founder of the Royal Society. There are many other fine memorials and statues worth inspection. On a sunny day brilliant shafts of light slant down from above, making the dark corners of this great building even more than usually silent and mysterious.

166. Monument to Viscountess Doneraile, by S. Vierpyl, St. Patrick's Cathedral

St. Stephen's, Mount Street Crescent

St. Stephen's, in the heart of the Pembroke Estate, was designed by John Bowden in the Greek Revival style, and completed after his death by Joseph Welland. It was opened in 1824, but since then the interior has been remodelled and it is now high Victorian. It contains the case of the Snetzler organ designed for the Rotunda Chapel in 1754. St. Stephen's closes the vista down one side of Merrion Square and Upper Mount Street, and is generally known as the 'pepper-pot' church.

167. St. Stephen's

The Front of S^t. Warburghs Church.

The Front of S^t. Warburghs Church.

168. Baroque façade of St. Werburgh's Brooking's Map, 1728

St. Werburgh's Church

St. Werburgh's Church, just outside the Castle walls, was used by the Viceroys until the Chapel Royal was built and the Viceregal pew may still be seen, decorated with the Royal Arms, just below the organ. St. Werburgh's has escaped nineteenth-century stained-glass gloom, and still preserves the cheerful atmosphere of an assembly room; moreover the recent restoration has been in the best possible taste. It has the finest Georgian church interior in Dublin and is open from 10 a.m.–4 p.m. (entry through a side door). The baroque façade by Burgh is all that remains of an earlier structure and dates from 1715. The upper half of this composition was removed after the '98 rebellion because it overlooked the Castle and the authorities feared that it presented a security risk. The interior dates from 1759 and was designed by John Smyth, who was building the Provost's House at the same time; there is excellent stucco in the chancel by Michael Maguire and the unusual gothic pulpit carved by Richard Stewart for the Chapel Royal has found a place here. Lord Edward FitzGerald lies buried in the vaults, and not far from him lies Major Sirr, the Town-Major who inflicted the wounds when arresting him from which Lord Edward eventually died.

169. St. Werburgh's today

170. Interior of St. Werburgh's

DOMESTIC BUILDINGS

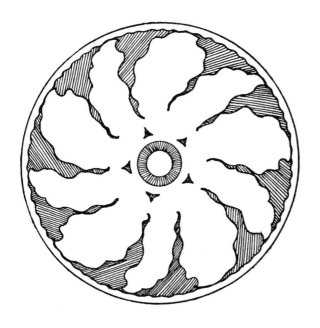

Aldborough House, North Circular Road

The last great stone mansion to be built in Dublin still stands by the 'five lamps' on the way to Malahide, and although the garden has been built over, the façade has recently been cleaned. Aldborough House is at present used as offices by the Post Office. The one surviving wing, originally built as a theatre, is now a store. The interior is plain, and there is no longer any evidence of the painted ceilings which were once a feature of the house. The identity of the architect remains a mystery. The Earl of Aldborough had, twenty years before, built a great house in Stratford Place, off Oxford Street, London—the family name was Stratford. His country seat in Ireland was Belan, Co. Kildare, designed by Richard Castle. Aldborough House was begun in 1792 and completed in 1798, but its builder died only three years later. The house he built shines like a jewel in an otherwise undistinguished part of the city, well looked after to the present day.

171. Aldborough House, the south wing

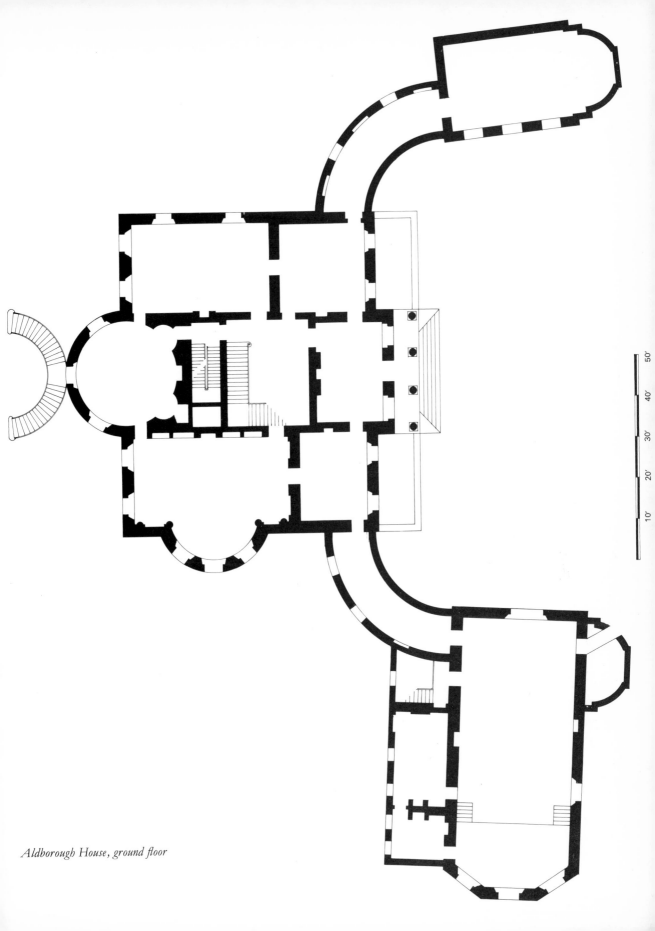

Aldborough House, ground floor

ALDBOROUGH-HOUSE   D U B L I N.

Will.ᵐ Skelton Sculp.ᵗ

Belvedere House, Great Denmark Street

Belvedere was completed in 1786 to the designs of Michael Stapleton, the architect and stuccodore, for the second Earl of Belvedere. It contains the outstanding Adam interior in Dublin, and now houses Belvedere College (which James Joyce attended) who take great pride in its splendour. The staircase is especially fine, picked out in several colours to show off the intricate patterns to best advantage, and the work beneath the staircase shows Stapleton at his most imaginative. The floor here was described in 1911 as being paved with 'black and white diagonal marble flagging'. The landing gives on to the Venus, Diana and Apollo rooms, all intricately decorated, and with some freehand modelling not often found at this late date.

174. Panel with stag in the Organ Room, Belvedere House

Charlemont House, Parnell Square
(the Lane Gallery of Modern Art)

Sir William Chambers designed Lord Charlemont's town house in 1767, and Gandon added on a library at the back which was demolished to make way for the art galleries in 1930. It contains the Irish share of the modern paintings left to Dublin by Sir Hugh Lane, the successful picture dealer and authority on art, who was also a substantial benefactor to the National Gallery of Ireland. The staircase and upstairs rooms retain many of their original features and are used for special exhibitions, and on the top floor there is an apartment for the curator.

Rutland Square, as it was known, was laid out by Dr. Mosse and used for concerts to raise money for the Rotunda Hospital. The view down over the square to the hospital, with its curved colonnades, must have been spectacular. Now it has been built over with a Nurses' Home and other buildings, as well as a memorial garden with formal water which has robbed the square of almost its last green open space.

176. Charlemont House

177. Lord Charlemont

178. Bossi mantelpiece,
Charlemont House

155

180. The cupola, Charlemont House

The Deanery, St. Patrick's Cathedral

The present Deanery dates from 1783
when it was rebuilt after a fire. Nothing
is left of Swift's Deanery, but to make
up for this a life-sized portrait of the
famous Dean, by Bindon, in an amazing
frame carved by John Houghton (for
£18 13s od) hangs in the dining room.
The porch was added in the nineteenth
century.

181. *Portrait of Swift by Bindon*
182. *Detail of side of frame of the Swift portrait*

183. *Detail of frame of the Swift portrait*

184. *Painting of the Duke of Buckingham, Viceroy, bust of Dean Ponsonby and bust of Swift (in the roundel) in the Deanery*

Ely House, Ely Place

Ely House faces down Hume Street to St. Stephen's Green, and dates from 1771, the year that its builder, Henry Loftus, was created Earl of Ely. Pronounced Eligh, it comes from Ely O'Carroll and not Ely in England. Originally a seven-bay house, it was divided in 1811 but without injuring the interior. The dining room has delicate plasterwork by Michael Stapleton, and the mantel plaque displays a sleeping Hercules. The same classical deity, life-size this time, greets the visitor at the foot of the stairs, where the Labours of Hercules are depicted as if climbing up to the *piano nobile*. From the ground up the figures represent the Erymanthian Boar, the Nemean Lion, the Cretan Bull, the Arcadian Stag, and Cerberus. They are carved in wood, gilded to look like metal. A statue of Christ looks down from the Venetian window at this strange procession. The inspiration came from a house in

185. Ely House

Brussels, built in 1731, which now houses the Musée Moderne; here the animals are cast in bronze.

The door furniture was taken from a design book by Robert Adam and the mantels and grates are still intact. It used to be possible to draw the bolt on the front door, by means of a wire, from a room upstairs. The Knights of Columbanus are the present owners of the house and sensible to its importance.

186. Plasterwork in the dining room of Ely House

187.(a) (b) and (c) The staircase at Ely House
depicting the Labours of Hercules

188. The statue of Hercules in the Musée Moderne, Brussels, which was the inspiration for the Hercules statue in Ely House

Iveagh House, St. Stephen's Green

Iveagh House, now the Department of External Affairs, incorporates two eighteenth-century houses, Nos. 80 and 81 St. Stephen's Green. No. 80 was the earliest house in Dublin by Richard Castle (1730) and some of the original features survive. When Sir Benjamin Guinness joined the two houses together he refaced them so as to look like one house; it was his grandson, the second Earl of Iveagh, who presented Iveagh House to the Irish Government

189. Mantelpiece in front hall, Iveagh House
190. Drawing room, Iveagh House

191. *Compartmented coved ceiling on the first floor of Iveagh House*

in 1939. It is mainly interesting today as having the most lavish Victorian ballroom in Dublin, complete with alabaster walls and a lincrusta ceiling designed by Young of London in 1863.

Sir Arthur Guinness, Lord Ardilaun, Sir Benjamin's eldest son, landscaped St. Stephen's Green and opened it to the public in 1877, until which time it had been reserved for local residents.

Leinster House, Kildare Street

Richard Castle designed the largest private house in Dublin for James FitzGerald, 20th Earl of Kildare, in 1745, and it was known as Kildare House until James became the first Duke of Leinster in 1766. He built it outside the then fashionable part of the city, and is supposed to have answered criticism by declaring 'wherever I go fashion will follow'. It has. Apart from the Senate Chamber, remodelled after designs by James Wyatt in 1780, and some compartmented ceilings by Sir William Chambers of 1767, the house has altered little. The great entrance hall takes up two storeys, and has the original mantel and black and white squared floor. The library, beneath the Senate, has a heavy compartmented ceiling; small wonder that Lord Edward FitzGerald found the house 'melancholy'. There is a good Francini figured ceiling on the ground floor, in what is now a reading room. The spiral staircase has been replaced by a lift.

192. Leinster House, from Rocque's Map of Dublin, 1756

There is an axial corridor dividing the house in two, as at Castletown, Co. Kildare, and the White House in Washington. Beside the plan of the White House by the hand of its Irish architect, James Hoban, is the section of a *three*-storey elevation very like Leinster House, with a rusticated ground floor and pilasters springing from it. This scheme was abandoned on General Washington's advice as being too costly, and the elevation of the White House does correspond with the two upper floors of Leinster House. Both owe much to James Gibbs' *A Book of Architecture* (1728), which Castle is likely to have owned, and which contains an elevation identical to the two upper floors of Leinster House.

193. Leinster House

194. (a) and (b)
Details of the Senate
ceiling, Leinster House

195. Entrance hall,
Leinster House

196. *Compartmented ceiling by William Chambers, Leinster House*

197. *Francini ceiling in the reading room, Leinster House*

198. Library, Leinster House

*199. Mantelpiece in
the garden hall,
Leinster House
200. Mantelpiece in
the library, Leinster
House*

The Mansion House, Dawson Street

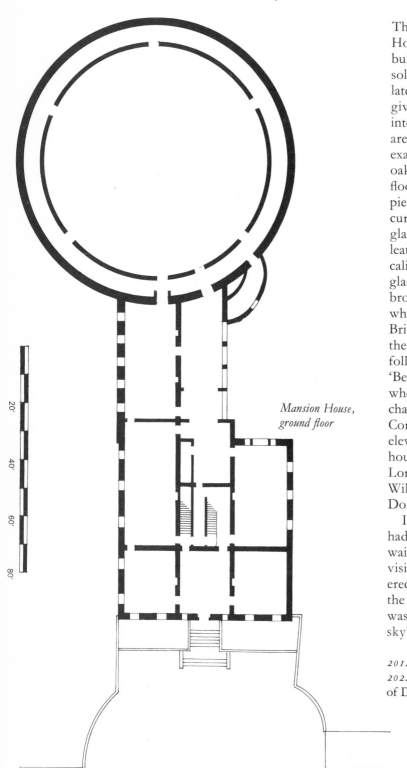

Mansion House, ground floor

The Victorian exterior of the Mansion House conceals the red brick house built by Joshua Dawson in 1710, and sold to Dublin Corporation five years later. The Committee's report of 1715 gives a detailed description of the interior: 'The rooms on the first floor are fourteen feet three inches high, all exactly well wainscotted with Danzick oak and French wallnut, with very good floors, locks and choice marble chimney pieces . . . tapestry hangings, silk window curtains and window seats and chimney glass in the great bed chamber; the gilt leather hangings, four pairs of scarlet caliminco window curtains and chimney glass in the wallnut parlour; . . .'. The bronze equestrian statue of George I which had stood on the old Essex Bridge was erected on the lawn beside the Mansion House in 1798, with the following inscription on the pedestal: 'Be it remembered that, at the time when rebellion and disloyalty were the characteristics of the day, the loyal Corporation of the City of Dublin re-elevated this statue of the illustrious house of Hanover—Thomas Fleming, Lord Mayor—Jonas Paisley and William Henry Archer, Sheriffs—Anno Domini, 1798'.

In 1821 the house was still brick, and had a ballroom fifty-five feet long wainscotted in Irish oak. For the King's visit that year a great Round Room was erected in which he was entertained by the Mayor and Corporation; the dome was 'painted to represent a beautiful sky'.

201. Mansion House
202. The Mansion House in Brooking's Map of Dublin, *1728*

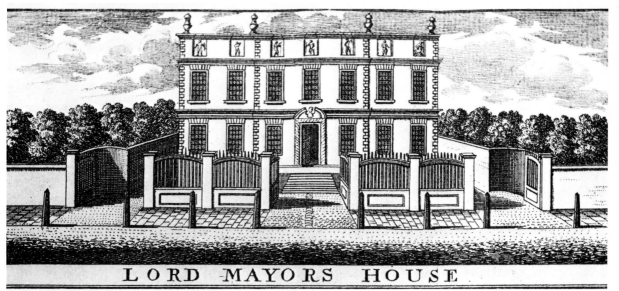

LORD MAYORS HOUSE

203. *The drawing room, Mansion House*

The Marino Casino, Clontarf

Two miles from Dublin, on the road to Malahide, stands the Marino Casino, a garden pavilion or literally 'small house' which was the first neo-classical building in Ireland. It was built for the Earl of Charlemont to the designs of Sir William Chambers from 1758 onwards, at the then enormous cost of £60,000. It stood in the grounds of Marino House, which has long since disappeared, and which had been Lord Charlemont's seaside villa where he could take the air and entertain in country surroundings. It was part of an elaborate landscaped park, with a rustic cottage, a gothic seat, and a lake, all of which have now gone. The Casino was originally conceived by Chambers as one of the end pavilions in his unexecuted design for Harewood, Yorkshire. At the four corners guardian lions, reminiscent of those beloved of Hubert Robert, keep a sleepy watch. These were carved by Joseph Wilton who also carved the magnificent Royal State Coach, designed by Chambers, at Buckingham Palace. The rest of the carved stonework was by Simon Vierpyl who was in charge of the building. Chambers never came to Ireland, but his correspondence shows the interest he took in every small detail of the Casino. Samples of the colours to be used were sent from England, and Chambers complained of the 'very considerable alteration in the colours before they arrive in Dublin'. There are two storeys over a basement, and long tunnels lead underground from the area, lit by overhead grills. There are no gutters or downpipes—the free-standing pillars at the corners are hollow and take the rainwater. The funereal urns on the parapet are in fact functional chimneys, and are echoed by those that adorn the Custom House designed by Chambers' pupil Gandon.

The interior has delicate plasterwork and inlaid floors of fine workmanship; there is a bedroom floor. A temporary canopy could be erected on the roof, whence a fine prospect of the bay of Dublin was obtainable.

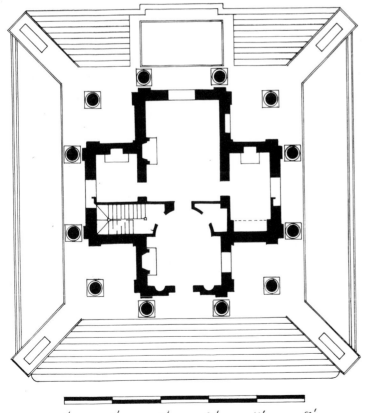

Marino Casino

204. Marino Casino
205. A guardian lion
at the Marino Casino

206. *Funereal urn on parapet of Marino Casino*
functions as a chimney
207. *Ornamental urn, Marino Casino*

Powerscourt House, South William Street

Powerscourt House was built in 1771 to the designs of Robert Mack and is one of the grandest stone houses in Dublin, seventy-three feet high, with a dining room thirty-six feet long. The granite for the front came from quarries on the family estate in Co. Wicklow. The façade is busy with ornament and rustication, and were it not for the gothic glazing bars in the arched windows, still to be seen in the basement, the house would appear to be of an earlier date. Diminutive curves to each side lead to monumental arches, which gave on to the kitchens and stables. These curves are not symmetrical, and drawing the ground plan of the house is a regular test at the architectural school. An attic with consoles surmounts the whole, which was intended as an observatory. The sides are of yellow and the back is of red brick, giving on to a courtyard designed by Francis Johnston as part of the Stamp Office which the house was to become after the Union.

The interior has been well preserved over the years by Messrs. Ferrier and Pollock, clothing wholesalers, who are the present owners. It has plasterwork in the rococo manner by James McCullagh, who charged £106 for the hall and £250 for the walls and ceiling of the staircase. Most of the reception rooms have Adamesque plasterwork by

208. Powerscourt House

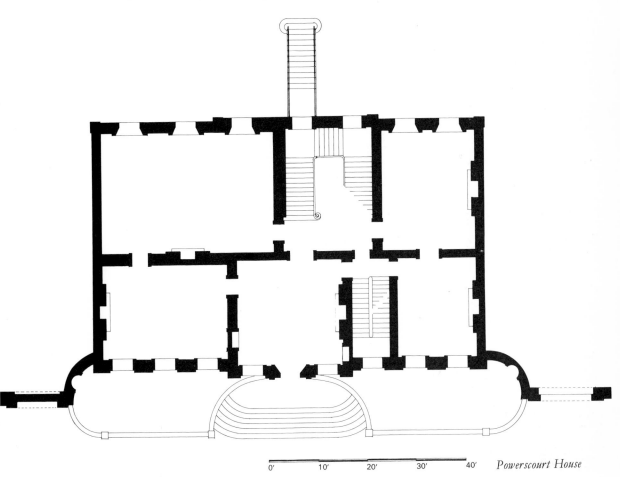

0' 10' 20' 30' 40' *Powerscourt House*

Michael Stapleton, who used the same plaques at 16 St. Stephen's Green. A delightful invention of his that is found here, at 17 St. Stephen's Green and at Lucan House, Co. Dublin, is a cross-vaulted ceiling dropped at the corners, giving the effect of a tent. The wood-carving is by Ignatius McDonagh, and is at its best on the mahogany staircase.

209. Plasterwork ceiling in Powerscourt House

210. Plasterwork on the staircase, Powerscourt House

Provost's House, Trinity College

The Provost's house enjoys the distinction of being the only great Dublin house still in use in the manner intended at the time it was built. Francis Andrews was made Provost of Trinity in 1758 and in the following year work started on his palatial new residence in the southwest corner of the College grounds. A handsome rusticated gateway near the foot of Grafton Street leads to the great grey house, its height accentuated by deferential one-storey wings. The central block is a copy of a house in London designed for General Wade by the 'Architect Earl', Lord Burlington, who had in his possession a drawing by Palladio from which the design was borrowed.

The architect was John Smyth (Dr. McParland doubts that he was capable of such an original and refined interior) who was responsible for the finest classical church façade in the city, St. Catherine's, Thomas Street. Smyth borrowed the elevation of the Redentore for St. Thomas's Church (since destroyed) and framed it with curved sweeps; he was evidently a dedicated Palladian.

The rhythm of the exterior arches and rustication is carried on into the entrance hall, where the walls are of wood cut to resemble stone as far as the springing of the arches. The outer, inner and staircase halls are paved in Portland stone edged in black. The staircase, lit by an immense arched window, has a handsome wrought-iron balustrade and leads up to a landing lit by an oval gallery and skylight above. The great saloon takes up the entire front of the house on the *piano nobile*. It is dominated by a full-length portrait by Gainsborough of the then Viceroy, the

211. The Provost's House from the Hibernian Magazine

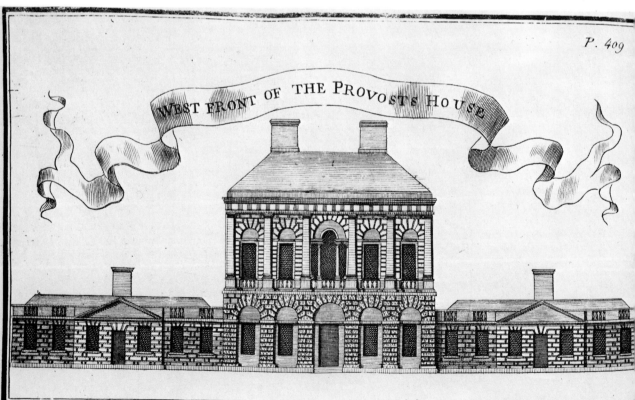

4th Duke of Bedford, the friend of Provost Andrews and Chancellor of the University. The coved and coffered ceiling, along with all the other plasterwork in the house, is the work of Patrick and John Wall. Most of the rooms have carved wood mantels stained dark to the colour of mahogany, an unusual feature. There is a good collection of paintings that was bequeathed to the College by the Reverend Samuel Madden.

212. The Provost's House entered through the gateway on Grafton Street

213. Provost's House hall

*214. Provost's House
staircase*

215. Saloon, Provost's House

216. Dining room, Provost's House

217. Small dining room, Provost's House

218. Drawing room, Provost's House

219. *Portrait of Hugh Boulter, Primate 1724–42,*
one of the collection of paintings in the Provost's
House

220. *The library,*
Provost's House

The Royal Irish Academy, No. 19 Dawson Street

The present house, which may
have been designed by John Ensor,
dates from 1769 when Lord Knapton of
Abbeyleix sold the old house, built in
1719, to Thomas Knox, who was
created Viscount Northland in 1791.
His son was made Earl of Ranfurly in
1831, but by this time the family had
sold the house to John Adrien (1810),
so it is known as Northland House to
this day. George Knox, M.P., Lord
Northland's son, was a friend of Wolfe
Tone and distinguished himself by a
speech on the Union, in which he
pointed out the disastrous effects of
such a measure, and warned the House
that a discontented and unguided
Ireland might one day 'become, in the
English speaking world, as formidable a
source of aggressive Jacobinism as
France had been on the continent'.

Gresham, the hotel-keeper of
Sackville (O'Connell) Street, bought the
house in 1835 and let it, first as a
Freemason's Tavern and later as a
Conservative Club. By 1845 it had
become the Irish Reform Club. The
Royal Irish Academy moved here in
1852 from Grafton Street. The house
has exceptionally fine plasterwork
similar to that at St. Vincent's Hospital,
with Berainesque frames and rather
primitive rococo decoration in the
Chinese taste. The Academy built its
reading room and meeting room over
the garden to the rear, so the Venetian
window on the staircase had to be
blocked up and a new window was
opened on the side wall. The rest of the
plaster in this house is transitional,
tending towards the geometrical in
design.

*221. Plasterwork on the walls and ceiling of the
Royal Irish Academy staircase*

222. Detail of the plasterwork, R.I.A.

Royal Irish Academy of Music, No. 36 Westland Row

No. 36 Westland Row was built in 1771 by Nicholas Tench of Fassaroe, Co. Wicklow for his own use. He also built Nos. 15 to 18 Ely Place and No. 2 Hume Street. It soon became the town house of the Earl of Conyngham, and subsequently that of Sir George Aylmer of Newcastle Lyons. Surgeon John

223. The Royal Irish Academy of Music, Westland Row

Hamilton was the inhabitant in 1844, and Captain John Aylmer in 1847. Mr. de Burgh of St. Doulough's was the last private owner; the Royal Irish Academy of Music purchased the house from him for £2,000 in 1871. In 1911 they also bought Nos. 38 and 39. The decoration is very delicate and some of the mouldings are made of pewter. There is an eccentric Gothic fireplace in the Organ Room, where Vestal Virgins feature in the plasterwork. Elsewhere the ornament is reminiscent of that of Belvedere House, Powerscourt House, and Clonmell House pointing to the authorship of Michael Stapleton.

224. Wrought ironwork on the staircase of the Academy of Music

225. Academy of Music: the main drawing room on the floor above street level

226. *Gothic fireplace in the Organ Room of the Academy of Music*
227. *Academy of Music: inlaid mahogany door with acanthus leaf surround modelled in pewter*

The *Former* Palace of St. Sepulchre, Kevin Street

The Protestant Archbishops of Dublin lived in St. Sepulchre's, overlooking St. Patrick's Cathedral, the Deanery and Marsh's Library, until the eighteenth century. One remaining carved doorcase *c.* 1600 gives an idea of how elaborate the interior must have been. It is now a Police Barracks.

228. Carved doorcase, Palace of St. Sepulchre's

No. 52 St. Stephen's Green

No. 52 St. Stephen's Green, like its sister house No. 53, was built in 1771 and they are very similar in design. David La Touche of the banking family lived here from the time it was built until his death in 1805, and the house has suffered little since then. It was restored in 1970 and is now the Dublin headquarters of the E.E.C.

Facing the front door are twin doric doorcases with broken pediments, one of which leads to the main staircase. On the wall to the right are the holders for Sedan chair poles. At the head of the stairs is the Music Room, with musical instruments in the plaster frieze and on the mantel. The walls were decorated by Peter de Gree, *c.* 1785, in green and white to match the Verd-antique marble mantel. The panels represent Apollo playing his lyre to attentive muses, Orpheus and Eurydice, a Nereid and

229. Front door, 52 St. Stephen's Green

other similar subjects interspersed with musical trophies. The back drawing room has a ceiling with a centrepiece painted by Angelica Kauffmann taken from Guido's Aurora, and painted doors probably by the same hand.

Kauffmann was in Ireland in the year the house was built, and was a friend of La Touche, so that of all the work attributed to her none has a better claim to be authentic.

230. Doorhandle and keyhole, 52 St. Stephen's Green

231. Music Room, 52
St. Stephen's Green

232. Musical themes in
the decoration of the
Music Room

233. *Drawing room of 52 St. Stephen's Green.*
Ceiling centrepiece by Angelica Kauffmann

No. 85 St. Stephen's Green *(Clanwilliam House)*

No. 85 St. Stephen's Green was built by Captain Hugh Montgomery in 1738 and was the first stone-fronted house on the Green. In 1785 it came into the possession of Viscount Clanwilliam and is still known as Clanwilliam House although it now forms part of Newman House and University College. The architect was Richard Castle, and the plasterwork by the Francini brothers is by far their most elaborate in Dublin.

234. Nos. 85 and 86 St. Stephen's Green

Dwarfed by its neighbours, No. 85 is larger than it appears and has a gothic extension at the back, *c.* 1780. It was built for entertaining rather than for living in: almost the whole house is given to reception rooms. The hall floor in black and white, the black hall mantel, the ironwork and carved mahogany staircase are of the highest quality. The Apollo Room is ornamented with plaster figures of

classical deities. Its only parallel in Ireland is the Francini dining room at Riverstown, Co. Cork.

The saloon takes up the entire front of the house on the floor above, the ceiling ornamented with plaster gods and goddesses in bold relief. A still more elaborate version of this design is the grandest baroque ceiling in Ireland, representing 'the courtship of the gods' at Carton, Co. Kildare, where the architect was also Richard Castle.

235. Plasterwork by Francini on the saloon ceiling, No. 85 St. Stephen's Green

236. Entrance hall, No. 85 St. Stephen's Green

No. 86 St. Stephen's Green

No. 86 was built in 1765 by Robert West for Richard Chapell Whaley, M.P., who was living in No. 85 while it was being built; it now forms part of Newman House. The plasterwork by Robert West is of exceptional quality, and ranks with No. 20 Lower Dominick Street as his best work. His particular hallmark, the bird, is found here in every conceivable attitude. He may have drawn his inspiration from the raucous seagulls that came up the Liffey with the sailing ships, as his yard or workshop was not far from the river.

Richard Chapell Whaley, nicknamed 'burn-chapel' for his priest-hunting activities, wrote a rhyming cheque in favour of his wife:

> *Mr. Latouche*
> *Open your pouch*
> *And give unto my darling*
> *Five hundred pounds sterling:*
> *For which this will be your bailey,*
> *Signed Richard Chapell Whaley.*

His son, the famous dare-devil 'Buck' Whaley, is best remembered for his wager to walk to the Holy Land. The journey cost him £8,000 and left him with a profit of £7,000, 'the only instance in all my life before, in which any of my projects turned out to my advantage!'

Beside No. 86 is the Byzantine entrance to the University Church, built by John Hungerford Pollen in 1855.

240. Plasterwork at No. 86 St. Stephen's Green

*Newman House: No. 85 St. Stephen's Green
(bottom) and No. 86 (top). Ground plan*

10'   20'   30'   40'   50'

241. *Plasterwork decoration of the staircase by Robert West, at No. 86 St. Stephen's Green*

242. *Detail of Robert West's plasterwork above the staircase window*

No. 6 South Leinster Street

This house was built *c.* 1755 in the manner of Richard Castle and has florid plasterwork by Robert West, akin to his work at Mornington House and No. 86 St. Stephen's Green. The earliest date at which Dublin street directories give the names of the occupiers of houses is 1834, and by that date the Stewarts of Killymoon, Co. Tyrone, were already in occupation. Tradition has it that this was the dower house of the Dukes of Leinster. The Stewarts were (and still are) bankers and agents for the Longford and de Vesci families. Martin Cregan, the portrait painter, who started life as a servant of the Stewarts, lived and worked here from 1822 to 1834; he was president of the Royal Hibernian Academy from 1832–1855. The house is well cared for by Asbestos Cement Ltd.

243. Plasterwork by Robert West on the landing ceiling, No. 6 South Leinster Street
244. No. 6 South Leinster Street

*245. Plasterwork on
the dining room ceiling*

*246. Detail of front
door, No. 6 South
Leinster Street*

*247. Mantelpiece,
No. 6 South Leinster
Street*

Tyrone House, Marlborough Street

Tyrone House was built for Sir Marcus Beresford, grandfather of the first Marquess of Waterford, in 1740 and was designed by Richard Castle. It was one of the city's first Palladian houses built of stone. The property, which had a park and garden of five acres, was sold to the Board of National Education in 1835. The new owners pulled down the stable block to the north and built a replica of the house so that it now has a twin, albeit a hundred years younger, standing beside it on Marlborough Street. The entrance front has been mutilated since Pool and Cash published the elevation in 1780; a clumsy portico has been added, and the Venetian window above has been squared off. The cut stone of the garden front,

248. The Earl of Tyrone's House

seldom seen, is very fine. There is a black Kilkenny marble mantel in the front hall, where these were often placed in houses designed by Castle, for instance at Russborough, Westport (recently removed) and No. 85 St. Stephen's Green. The massive mahogany staircase with its doric balusters resembles the one at Russborough so closely that it must be by the same hand. The floor of the staircase hall is mahogany laid on a diagonal pattern. Massive mahogany doors and panelling up to dado level are to be found throughout the house, providing a steady anchor for the dramatic plaster flourishes above. The plasterwork on the staircase incorporates female heads framed in

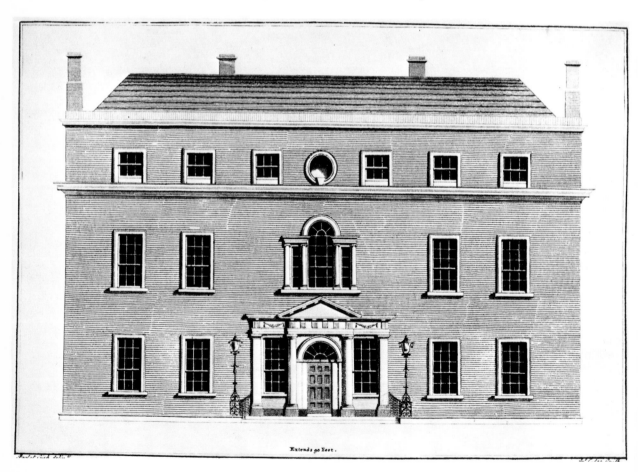

giant shells that are identical to the heads on the wall of the saloon at Carton, Co. Kildare, where the Francini brothers were responsible for the great baroque ceiling in 1739, under the direction of the same architect. A comparison of the frieze in the saloon or principal drawing room at Carton and at Russborough with that at Tyrone House leaves no doubt that the Francini were responsible for all three.

One room was hung with tapestries after the younger Teniers, probably the room now used by the Minister for Education. The panelling here has curious curl graining, made by cutting the mahogany at the junction of two large branches, and giving the effect of walnut. The saloon is a few feet higher than the other reception rooms leading to it; as a result, a windowless servants' room on the bedroom floor above was reached by steps up the coving.

Tyrone House

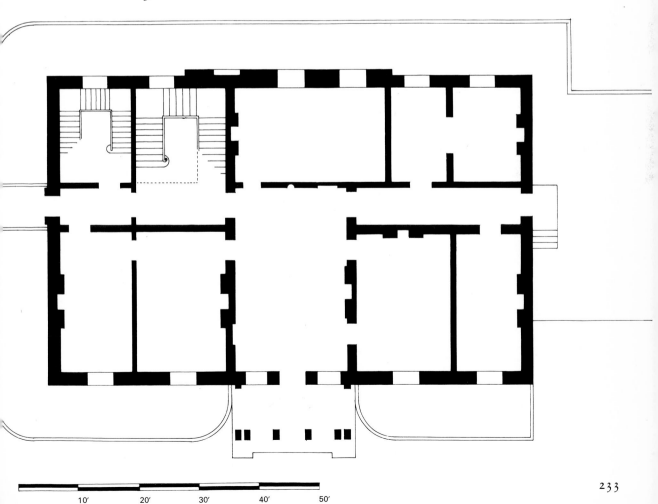

10'   20'   30'   40'   50'

234

249. Plasterwork on the landing, Tyrone House   *250. Detail of the saloon ceiling, Tyrone House*

ENDPAPERS: *Béranger
Toile of Lord
Charlemont*